IN BLACK AND WHITE

A COMPREHENSIVE COLLECTION OF THE MILLINERY ENGRAVINGS FROM *GODEY'S LADY'S BOOK* AND *PETERSON'S MAGAZINE*

VOLUME 2: HEAD-DRESSES AND NETS
1860-1865

WITH ADDITIONAL ENTRIES FROM THE LADY'S HOME MAGAZINE, AND THE LADY'S FRIEND

COMPILED BY DANNIELLE PERRY
AND MANDY FOSTER

WWW.TIMELYTRESSES.COM

In Black and White
A COMPREHENSIVE COLLECTION OF THE MILLINERY ENGRAVINGS FROM GODEY'S LADY'S BOOK AND PETERSON'S MAGAZINE
Volume II: Head-Dresses and Nets
1860-1865

©2015 Timely Tresses

ISBN-13: 978-1508687894

ISBN-10: 1508687897

In Black and White

In addition to the color plates in the fashion magazines, most magazines had black and white engravings in each issue and a section describing the latest fashions. Black and white engravings were often fashion forward compared with the color plates perhaps due the time intensive process of coloring. For example, high brim bonnets are regularly seen in the black and white plates for 1862 while only rarely in the color plates. The same is true for 1864 where the black and white engravings precede the color plates in showing the Fanchon and Empire styles of bonnets. As with the color plates, the engravings repeat.

About the project.

I started this project in 2006 when Mandy Foster and I started Timely Tresses. At that point, I had only three years of bound lady's magazines and a collection of individual fashion plates. Eager for information on bonnets, I combed the pages of the magazines for engravings and descriptions. Eventually, Mandy and my collection of lady's books expanded to include all of the *Godey's Lady's Books* from 1831-1877 and all of the *Peterson's Magazines* from 1845-1877. When we started our collections, the plan was to carefully index and scan each magazine for easy reference. However, life and kids happen. We made it through the color fashion plates and then petered out.

I revisited the project in 2011 when I wrote *Fashionable Bonnets.* The intention then was to catalogue all the information from 1854-1865 from *Godey's* and *Peterson's* and publish it as a companion to *Fashionable Bonnets.* Of course, whenever I start a project I never think it is going to be as time consuming as it proves to be.

I recently purchased a hand-held scanner and promised myself to finish this work. I scanned all of the black and white millinery engravings from 1860-1865 from the original books at 300dpi or more. Mandy and I transcribed all of the millinery descriptions and relative information using fonts as close as possible to the original fonts. We used the spacing, italics, and odd spellings as present in the original volumes. One of my biggest pet peeves is when people call bonnets hats and hats bonnets, well, they did it in the 19th century too. We used our best judgment differentiating the descriptions of each when no engraving was provided. Our intention is to complete companion volumes for these books for children's clothing, music, and other wardrobe items. We will see how that goes. You might have to wait until our children leave for college.

This is a reference work about the books only. We have not contributed any information on the making or shapes of original bonnets. We have not included any original photographs. The purpose is to have the information easily accessible without having to touch the original books.

Sharing of information is important to me. I hope you enjoy this volume be it for personal enjoyment or recreating 19th century millinery.

Dannielle

HEADDRESSES

GODEY'S LADY'S BOOK
JANUARY 1860

CHITCHAT UPON NEW YORK AND PHILADEL-
PHIA FASHIONS FOR JANUARY.

For the wedding-ball, which would be the prelude to several other large parties, Mme. Bonier-Cherre supplied some very beautiful articles. Her Alma coiffure of white lilac in very small branches, mixed with roses, and forming a bow at the side, from which escaped two unequal branches of lilac foliage ; and her Aïssa coiffure, composed of two garlands of rose-leaves, one of which lies on the forehead, the other on the back hair, the second row or-namented at the side with a long tuft of mixed roses, and the first row—that on the fore-head—having merely on the right a very small bunch of rosebuds. These two creations, quite new and exquisitely graceful, will be worn by two cousins of the bride, who bear one of the great historical names of France.

Other coiffures, still more decidedly oriental, are: A gold diadem, with a large tuft of red ros-es and coffee-berries. A bow of flame-colored velvet and caraib fruit berries mixed up with gold lace and velvet poppies.

PETERSON'S MAGAZINE
JANUARY 1860

HEAD-DRESS.

FIG. IX.—HEAD-DRESS OF BLACK VEL-
VET, composed of loops, bows, and ends.

HEADDRESSES NECK-TIE, AND FANCY CUFF.

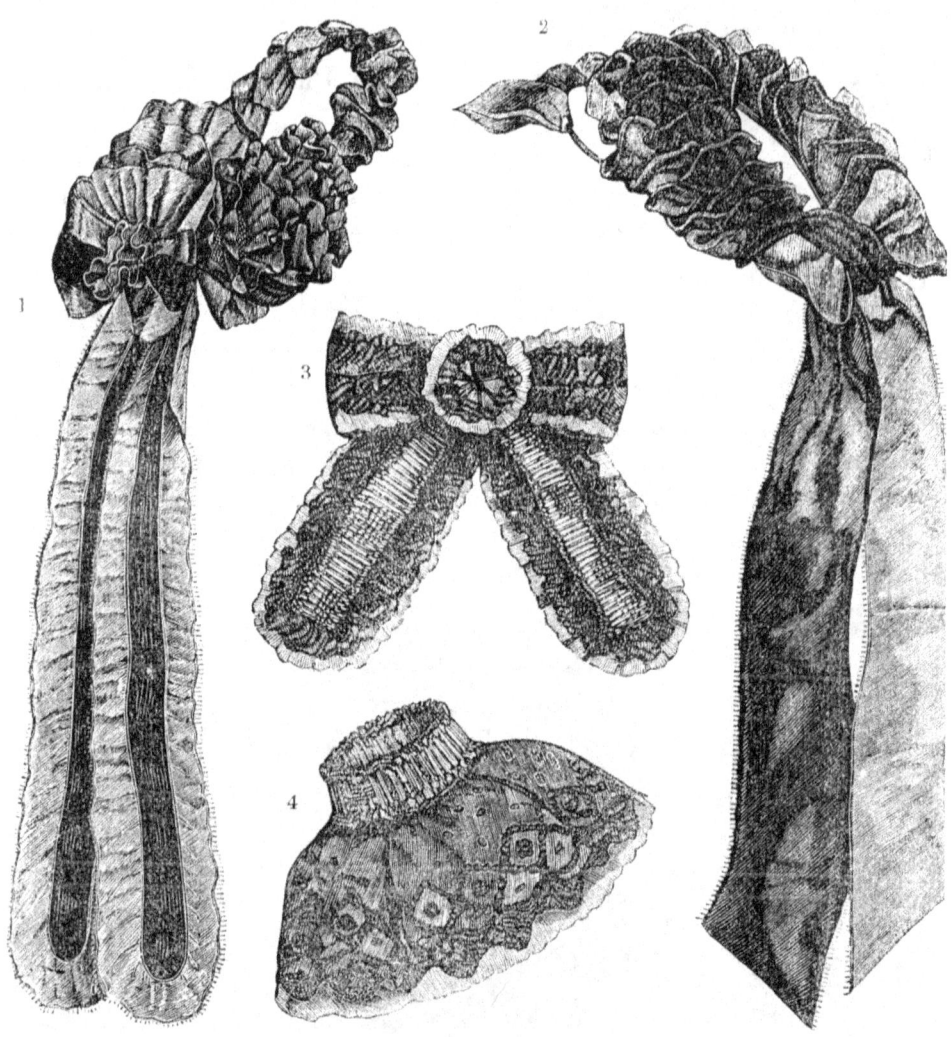

No. 1.—This headdress is quite novel; it is formed of ribbon, about and inch wide, drawn on one side to form a ruffle, and then sewed on in the style given in the engraving. For the bow, a velvet ribbon is required, and the drawn ribbon is placed on the edge of it, producing a very pretty effect.

No 2.—This is one of the latest styles of headdresses, and is exceedingly simple, being formed only of loops of black velvet and some fancy-colored ribbon, with a large bow at the back, and one streamer of black velvet and one of ribbon. This headdress fits on the back of the head ; but a roll of velvet rests on the front part of the head, and directly in the centre of it a bow is placed. This roll and bow can be omitted if it is not becoming, and still the headdress will be very pretty.

CHITCHAT UPON NEW YORK AND PHILADELPHIA FASHIONS FOR FEBRUARY.

Headdresses are still mostly of the fancy kind, and very elegant and graceful. One is formed of three squares of black velvet, bordered by a narrow gold fringe, and connected together by a torsade, from which hang three gold tassels. Another is composed of a torsade of flame-color velvet, with a broad and rounded end, and edged with blonde falling on the right hand side over a long velvet string. A small crown, rather inkling to the left side, is bordered there by a branch bearing bunches of red velvet flowers and beautiful aquatic leaves. A crown of China-rose chrysanthemums enveloped with openwork thulle composes a coiffure of vapory lightness, which is extremely becoming. One of these coiffures, which met with great success at Compeigne, is a headdress of white narcissuses mixed with bunches of gold elder-berries, while behind there is a plaited point of peach-bloom velvet, fastened by gold stars, and edged with small gold balls like those on the bunches. Torsades and plaits of velvet, in every variety of color, with bunches of gold or silver wheat-ears, make very beautiful diadems for young and pretty heads. Another little headdress consists of caul of black thulle, covered with crossings of velvet and worn quite at the back of the head. This caul is encircled with black lace which falls over the neck in the manner of a bavolet. At each side bouquets of flowers are fixed by pearl pins.

PETERSON'S MAGAZINE
FEBRUARY 1860

HEAD-DRESS OF CHENILLE AND GOLD CORD.
BY MRS. JANE WEAVER

THIS consists of a loop of chenille and gold lace twisted four-fold. The ends of the long tassels, as well as their upper setting, are of gold cord.

GENERAL REMARKS.—HEAD-DRESSES.—A delicious little head-dress for an evening party has a spiral, snail-shaped crown of mallow ribbon and a blonde lace laid on flat, forming a slight point on the forehead, and having under it a narrow pinked ruche like those on the head. On each side at the cheeks are loops of mallow ribbon, and two barbs of blonde are added behind on long ribbon strings which hang below them. Another head-dress is composed of two lozenges of velvet bordered with lace, one being placed very forward, the other behind on the back hair. These two lozenges are connected by a flame-color velvet torsade covered by a row of lace, and on the left side, under this torsade, is placed a branch of cherry-color magnolias blended with grass and reeds.

The other formed by a broad band of blue velvet, the ends of which are turned underneath, while the band itself is placed very low as a *cache-peigne*. In front of this band are two loops of blue ribbon, lying round on the head, while a gold torsade winds round them and terminates, on the one hand, in three hand- some tassels, and on the other in a branch of white and gold bell-flowers.

THE LADY'S HOME MAGAZINE
MARCH 1860

Head dresses are very plain, consisting of a *cache –peigne* of a couple of roses each side of the knot of hair, far back on the head, or a simple garland of spring flowers. White nar- cissas and rosebuds are in favor.

THE LADY'S HOME MAGAZINE
APRIL 1860

HEAD DRESS.

HEAD-DRESS.

GODEY'S LADY'S BOOK
MAY 1860

Fig. 2.   Fig. 3.   Fig. 4.

Figs. 2 and 3—Headdresses for dinner or evening company, suitable for a concert-room.

Fig. 2 is *en rosette* of a good lace point, starting from two flat bows of mauve-colored ribbon.

Fig. 3. is of Napoleon blue velvet and white thulle, with a cross wreath of blush roses and foliage.

Fig 4.—Headdress for evening. A cordon or wreath of delicate flowers above the forehead; at the back of the head, a cluster of large black roses without foliage, encircled by a barbe of black Chantilly lace, with loops of rose-colored satin ribbon.

CHITCHAT UPON NEW YORK AND PHILADEL-PHIA FASHIONS, FOR MAY.

The newest headdresses we have seen consist of four rosettes made of a ribbon of about an inch in width, box plaited and sewed on a piece of net to form a very full rosette ; two smaller rosettes go under the coil of hair, and two larger ones at the sides of the head ; they are made of two colored ribbons, two rosettes being of one color and two of another. Many have a band of ribbon about half an inch wide attached to the rosettes, going round the head and on one side ; about an inch from the middle part is placed a bow of ribbon.

THE LADY'S HOME MAGAZINE
MAY 1860

HEAD DRESS.

PETERSON'S MAGAZINE
MAY 1860

HEAD-DRESS.   HEAD-DRESS.

GODEY'S LADY'S BOOK
JULY 1860

Fig. 1.

THE LADY'S HOME MAGAZINE
JUNE 1860

Fig. 1.—Headdress of lace, ribbon, and flowers, The cap has a flounce which forms the curtain ; a knot of ribbon on the top, and a bouquet of golden coreopsis, with streamers of ribbon, make sufficient trimming.

PETERSON'S MAGAZINE
JULY 1860

GENERAL REMARKS.—HEAD-DRESSES.— Among the head-dresses lately imported, there is one consisting of a bandeau of black and violet velvet powdered with gold stars, and accompanied by two tufts, one very compact, of silk violets, and the other of black and violet bows mixed with gold threads. Another is a torsade of wide mallow ribbon blended with black lace, and fastened at the side by an agrafe of wheat-ears in silver.

LA BELLE.

(See description, page 191.)

HEADDRESSES.

La Bell.—This is a very simple and becoming headdress. It is made of narrow chenille, edged with large black beads, and underneath the chenille net, at the sides, are loops of ribbon ; at the back is a a bow with long ends.

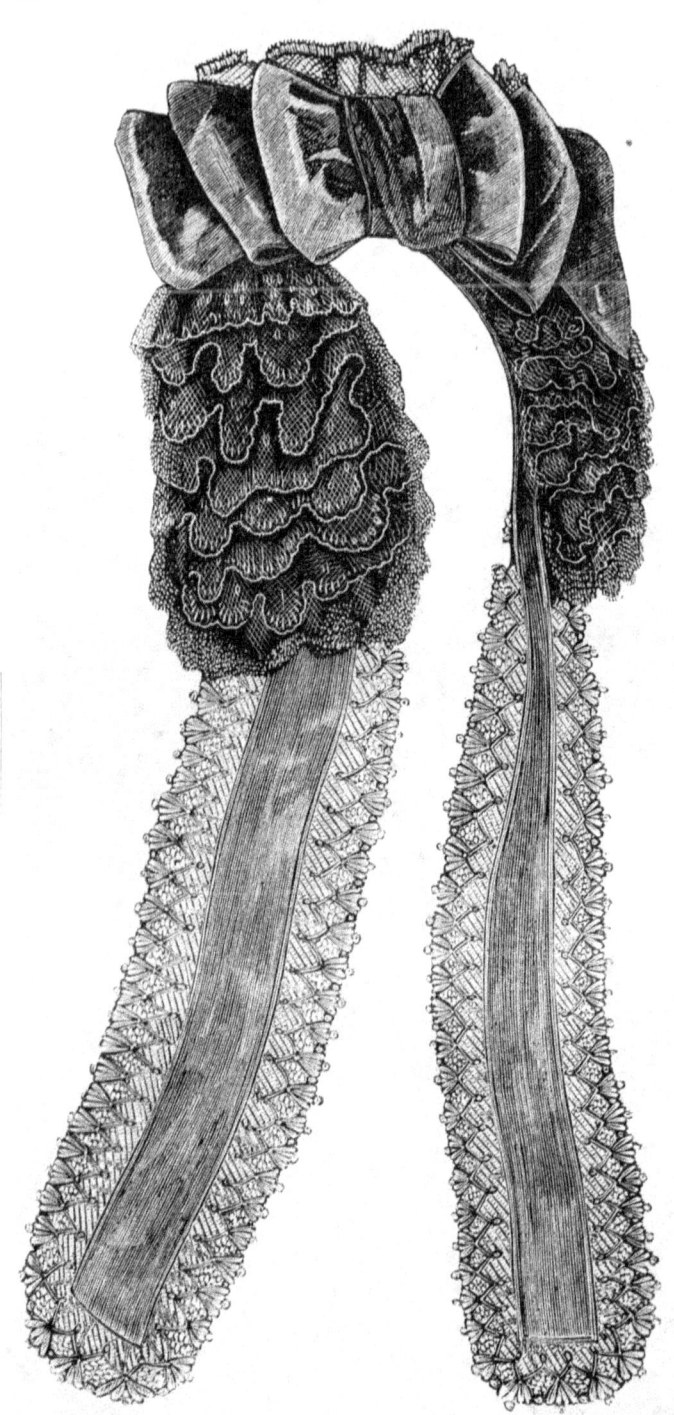

LA MATRONE.—*(See description, page 191.)*

La Matrone.—This headdress is very convenient for persons who are a little bald on the top of the head, as it is to be worn quite far over the head as a cap, but at the same time does not conceal the back hair. It is made of ribbon and lace.

LA PRINCESSE.

(See description, page 191.)

103

La Princesse.—This style of headdress is exceedingly pretty for young ladies, as it is so very simple. It is formed of plaits of narrow velvet and a bow of wide ribbon.

Fig. 5.

CHITCHAT UPON NEW YORK AND PHILADELPHIA FASHIONS FOR SEPTEMBER.

Several new coiffures, suitable for full evening-dress have just appeared. One consists of a very souple gold net. It droops, loose and flowing, over the back of the head, somewhat in the fanchon form, and it is edged round with small light tassels and pendeloques of gold. At the top, in front, there is a small bouquet of roses without foliage, and a bow of black velvet. A headdress without foliage, and a bow of black velvet. A headdress just received from Paris, where it is styled the *Coiffure Eugenie*, is in the form of a diadem or coronet, and consists of green velvet foliage, daisies white and colored with ornaments of gold intermingled. The coiffure *Louis Treize* is a toque of mauve-color velvet, ornamented with amethyst and a white ostrich feather. One of the prettiest of these headdresses is composed of blue velvet with a large agrafe of silver, and small silver chains disposed in festoons and pendant ends. Another consists of crimson velvet, and aigrette of white feathers, and tassels of gold. The *Coiffure Zouave* is in green velvet and gold, with a bandeau formed of white ostrich feathers twisted together.

Fig.5.—An unusually simple and tasteful headdress for the evening ; velvet ribbon, arranged as net, covers the twist, and has low flowing ends with tassels to the right ; to the left is placed a full blown rose, with foliage and drooping buds ; a cordon of buds and foliage on a velvet bandeau, crosses the hair.

GODEY'S LADY'S BOOK
NOVEMBER 1860

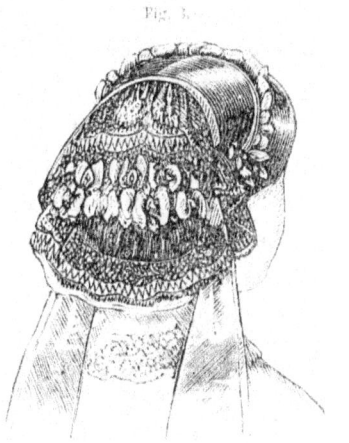

Fig. 3. Headdress of black lace and ribbon, for dinner and evening wear.

PETERSON'S MAGAZINE
NOVEMBER 1860

GENERAL REMARKS.—HEAD-DRESSES.— Among the evening coiffures most recently introduced in Paris, we have observed one formed of a net of chenille, and having on each side barbes of black lace square at the ends. A very pretty head-dress consisting of vine-leaves and clusters of blue grapes, with red velvet intertwined, is fixed at the back of the head by a bow of red velvet. Coiffures of the style just mentioned may be worn with black, white, or gray dresses. A much admired head-dress is composed of several small rosettes of blue ribbon, fixed low at the back of the head by a larger bow, which forms a *chignon*.

GODEY'S LADY'S BOOK
DECEMBER 1860

black lace at each end, with a gilt or jet pin knob in the centre.

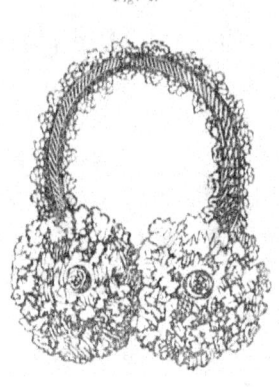

Fig. 1.—Headdress for dinner, or a reception. Barbes of ribbon and white lace, the lace barbe being made by uniting a wide edging; loops of groseille ribbon; rosettes of groseille velvet ribbon.

Fig. 3. Evening headdress. A circular band of green velvet, on which are placed thick rosettes of black lace ; jet drops fall from the lower portion of the wreath thus formed.

Fig. 4.—Band of fuschsia-colored velvet, edged on each side with black lace ; a rosette of

Fig. 5.—Cordon and flat bows for the hair, of black velvet and gold-colored ribbon. It is a good and becoming headdress.

CHITCHAT UPON NEW YORK AND PHILADELPHIA FASHIONS FOR JANUARY.

For all light tissues, flowers or foliage in bouquets, wreaths, agrafes, etc., are the most suitable ornaments. A parne of flowers is often almost as costly as one of gems, and includes whole set—wreath for the hair, bouquet de corsage, and sprays for the skirt of the dress. A parne of these fragile but exquisite ornaments often costs from $15 to $100, if ordered from the best French houses ; but their delicacy is so exquisite as to outrival nature. They may be set in any form most becoming to the wearer. It is absurd to wear a coronal, when a drooping wreath is more becoming, merely because people tell you "round wreaths are the most fashionable:" our steel-plate illustrates this ; and the best artistes mount a wreath for the face that is to wear it. We may notice among the infinite varieties of styles and blossoms a round headdress of convolvulus, with drooping branches all round, as well as the agrafes of the dress, which came from the celebrated flower manufactory of *Tilman*, 104 *rue de Richelieu*. Another headdress composed of China rose-color auriculas, divided into small tufts, accompanied a dress of China rose-silk. One, very light, was made of clematis and orange-bloom: it presented on the forehead a narrow but rounded cordon, which increased in volume behind. Another was composed of periwinkles, white lilac, and waxed orange-bloom. Both were master-pieces of taste. Bouquets to match, of an elongated form, were placed at the side of the waist. Mme. de Laère had also supplied a delightful coronet, formed of pale blue corn-flowers on the right, wheat-ears pointing upwards on the left, and, behind, a large tuft of wheat-ears and blue flowers. Last of all one of cherry-color wild roses and white lilac, extremely fresh and graceful.

When the dress is of a heavier fabric, the ornaments for the hair, which are now so popular, in gilt, etc., are very suitable ; also, headdresses combining velvet and flowers of the same material, velvet and gilt, etc.

For a dress of cerise and white, for instance, large cherry-color roses with fancy foliage, daisies, lilac velvet pansies and gold anemones. A large gold torsade incloses it on one side, and a bunch of white lilac hangs down on the other.

For a cherry-color dress covered with a white tulle tunic, a coiffure presenting a cherry velvet torsade fastened by three gold buckles, and terminated on one side by a tuft of white frizzed feathers, on the other by a large bow of two loops blended with another of gold cord, the two long tassels of which hung down on the shoulder.

Lastly, for two toilets of court mourning, the following headdresses:—

A bandeau of black and violet velvet powdered with gold stars and accompanied by two tufts, one very compact, of silk violets, and the other of black and violet bows mixed with gold threads. A torsade of wide mallow ribbon blended with black lace, and fastened at the side by an agrafe of wheat-ears in silver.

GODEY'S LADY'S BOOK
FEBRUARY 1861

Fig. 3

PETERSON'S MAGAZINE
MARCH 1861

GENERAL REMARKS.—A very simple head-dress can be arranged with a coronet of ruched black lace and a large bow of the same material placed just in the front. This head-dress can be finished off on one side by a bouquet of carnations, and on the other by a bow of ribbon the same color as the flowers.

HEADDRESSES.

(See description, Fashion Department.)

Fig. 1.

Fig. 2.

HEADDRESSES.

Fig. 1.—Coiffure of pieces of black velvet, trimmed with either black or white lace, and formed into a wreath, caught in front and back by pendants of black and gold bugles.

Fig. 2.—Net formed of narrow black velvet, fastened with jet beads, and trimmed with loops of black ribbon worked with jet beads ; a velvet bow with jet buckle finishes this wreath of loops in the centre.

Fig. 3.—Delicate wreath in white velvet leaves, with plumy, feathery pendants. It is intended to surround the hair, and fall on the neck. This is a graceful style of mounting for any kinds of leaves—a floral ornament now greatly used.

Fig. 4. Quiet and ladylike headdress, suited for a dinner or small evening party. Black velvet, jet slides, a fall of black lace ; to the right, a bow of black velvet ribbon with flowing ends ; to the left, a full blown rose, with trailing foliage.

GODEY'S LADY'S BOOK
JUNE 1861

CHITCHAT UPON NEW YORK AND PHILADELPHIA FASHIONS FOR JUNE.

Bridal Wreaths still affect the round form, slightly elongated before and behind. The last creations of Mme. Bonier-Cherre were, first, one of Lilac and orange-flower, coming rather low at the sides ; then one of narcissuses and orange-flower ; and lastly, one of orange-flower and jessamine. We have seen a few entirely of some large white flower, like the narcissus, the pink, or the primrose, and having only a tuft of orange-flowers added on one side.

The general form of headdresses partakes rather of the diadem and the *câche peigne*, connected by a very slender wreath on each side. The newest wreaths are composed of two sorts of flowers ; we notice some very pretty ones for young ladies ; one in which violets were blended with roses. In front was a round tuft of rosebuds, and behind a similar tuft in the middle of a double cordon of violets, made to part so as either to inclose the hair or to be placed underneath. Another wreath was of tea roses and pansies, and another of pinks mixed with grapes and geraniums with foliage.

PETERSON'S MAGAZINE
JUNE 1861

GENERAL REMARKS.—HEAD-DRESSES are still worn, the latest style being the coronet form. One of the prettiest which we have seen was made of ruched white tulle, with black velvet heartsease, embroidered gold, mingled with the ruching. Two lappets were fastened by a very large heartsease also embroidered in gold, which formed a cache-peigne behind. A single stud or ornament in the middle, is a very stylish coiffure, and very becoming to some faces. Black velvet coronets, with gold wheat-ears, made pretty head-dresses and may be worn in slight mourning.

GENERAL REMARKS.—LITTLE HEAD-DRESSES of ruched black lace, mixed with poppies, roses, and cornflowers, are still worn, with a black velvet bow and long ends behind.

VELVET HEAD-DRESS.

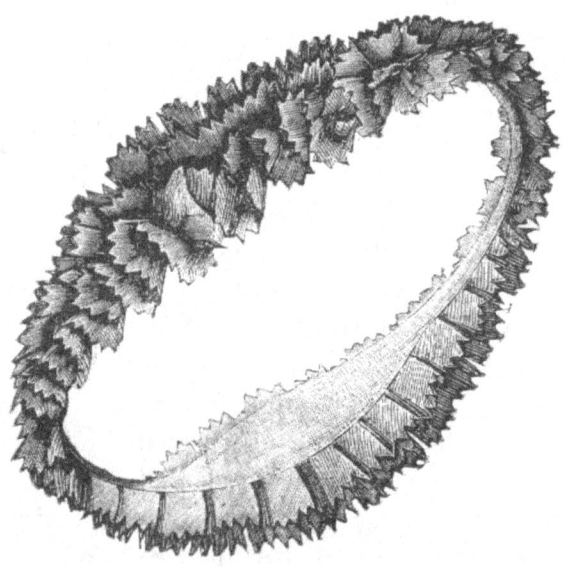

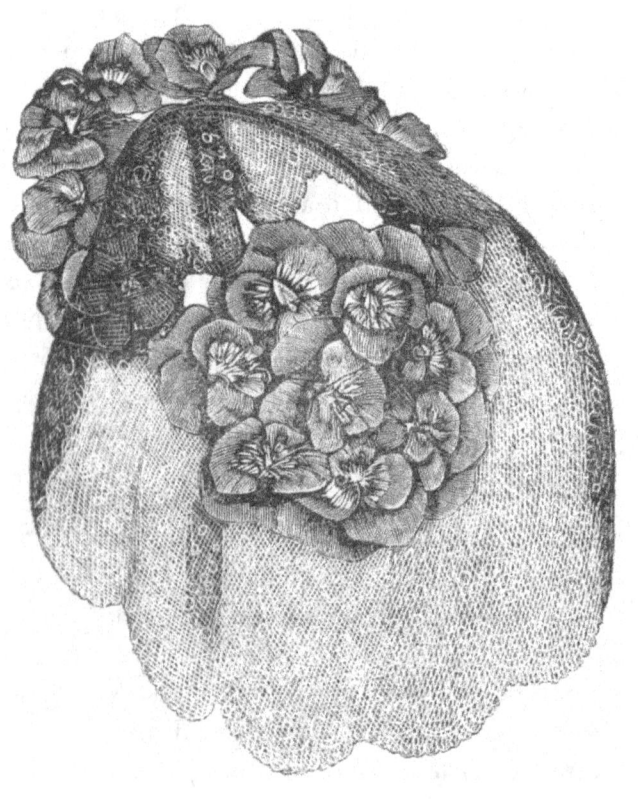

Fig. 5.

Fig. 5.—Headdress for evening wear ; a full wreath of daisies mounted with rose-colored ribbon, a flat bow of the ribbon on the forehead, with a bow and flowing ends behind.

Fig. 3.

Fig. 3.—Headdress of *tulle de soie*, black velvet, and full blush roses with foliage. The hair is turned back from the forehead, and the headdress set well on the back of the head.

CHITCHAT UPON NEW YORK AND PHILADELPHIA FOR SEPTEMBER.

One of her (Mme. Alexandrine) richest headdresses is a torsade of flame-colored ribbon ornamented on the right hand side with a knot of gold wheat ears and behind by a smaller knot from which a long white feather falls toward the left. One was quite round, of camellias of equal size ; another composed of a torsade of black velvet starred with gold and intertwined with a gold cord, terminated on the right hand side in two handsome tassels and dandelion puffs spangled with gold ; another was of red and white pinks mixed with fern-leaves ; another of large blue hortensias with silver hearts ; another of red hyacinths with pale foliage ; another of a *Magenta* velvet torsade, a Chinese tassel and gold chains ; another of pansies and tea-roses ; another of blue and white ribbon rolled with a silver torsade and having two silver tassels and blonde agrafes. We have never known headdresses so universally adopted, from the simple lace barbe to the artistic creations of Alexandrine or the importations of Madame Tighlman. We noticed this particularly in the review of a trousseau prepared recently for a lady of this city. The morning caps and headdresses formed a conspicuous and expensive part of the preparations. Each dress had its appropriate accompaniment. The mob, or Charlotte Corday cap, was the shape selected for morning wear ; to be adopted as soon as mademoiselle could write herself madame... Among other novelties, the most dainty of nightcaps had a bow exactly on the top, quite forward, of mauve-colored ribbon .

HEADDRESSES.

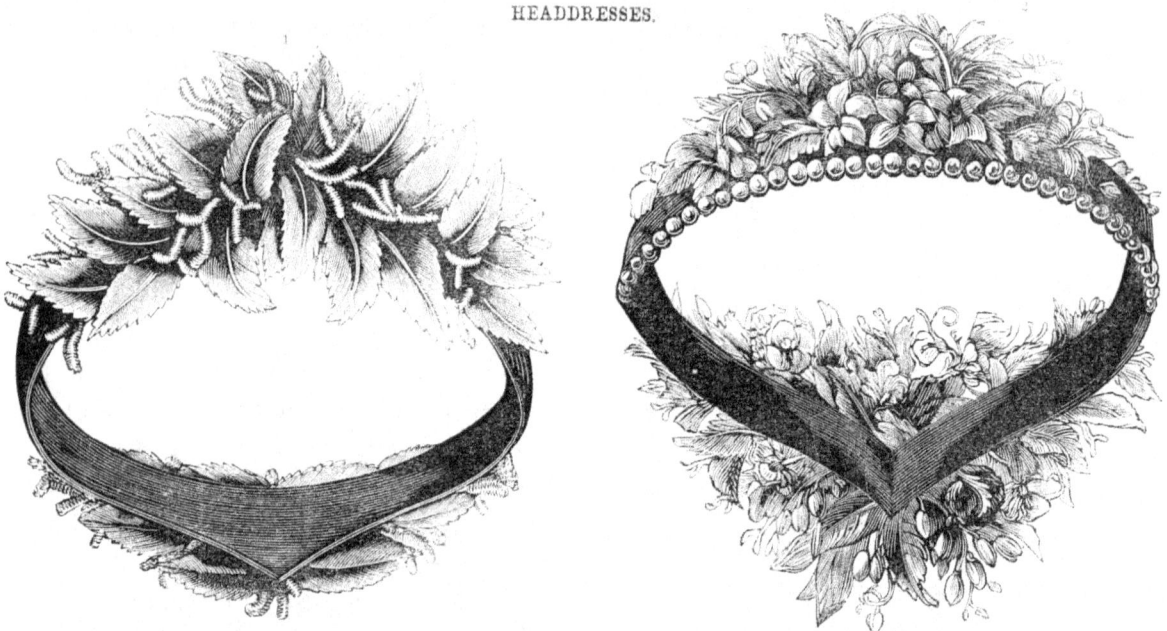

Fig.1.—This coiffure is composed of a black velvet coronet standing high in the front, and is trimmed with black velvet leaves veined with gold, and mixed with gold tendrils or sprigs. To make the coronet, procure twenty four inches of common chip or straw, one inch wide ; sew a thin wire on each side ; tack over this a piece of lining, and stretch the velvet tightly over it, stitching it neatly down on the wrong side. The leaves, which may be purchased in sprays, as also the gold tendrils, should then be prettily mounted on the coronet, leaving the latter without any trimming whatever at the sides. Our illustration shows the back of the headdress.

Fig.2.—This headdress may be made of artificial flowers, or pearl flowers and leaves mounted on wire. The coronet is composed of black velvet, with a row of large pearls fastened on the inner edge, the flowers being tastefully arranged high in the centre, and narrowing towards the sides, with a full bunch behind.

Fig. 9.

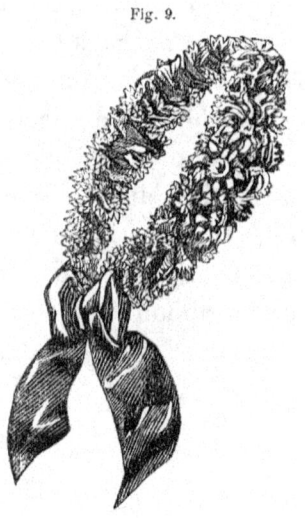

Fig. 9.—Wreath for dinner toilet, made of black lace and flowers, fastened at the back with black velvet bows and ends.

Fig. 10.

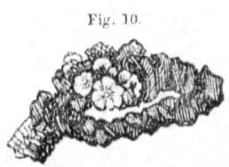

Fig. 10—Simple headdress of black ribbon, black lace, and purple pansies.

FIG. VI.—HEAD-DRESS, composed of black
lace and crimson ostrich feathers.

Fig. 2.

Fig. 3.

Fig. 4.

Fig. 2.—Headdress of lace, ribbon and flowers, for dinner or evening wear.

Fig. 3.—Headdress for concerts, opera, or party going. A caul or net for the hair, made of pearl beads, and ornamented at the top by a loop of larger beads, fastening drooping sprays of wheat. A wreath of black silk or velvet loops starts from each side the caul, and encircles the head ; pearl beads are wound through the loops.

Fig. 4.—headdress of braided ribbon, with a net foundation underneath to keep it in place. There is a spray of golden acorns and oak leaves in the centre, and to the left, quite low down, a bouquet of crimson velvet convolvulus, with leaves and tendrils, a few golden acorns showing at one side.

PETERSON'S MAGAZINE
NOVEMBER 1861

GENERAL REMARKS.—HEAD-DRESSES.— Many of the prettiest caps are formed of a combination of black and white lace. In Paris, peacocks' feathers have been a good deal used for evening head-dresses. They are worn above the forehead, mounted in the diadem form. Sometimes they are made into wreaths, which encircle the hair at the back of the head, and many headdresses are composed of peacocks' feathers intermingled with black lace. The newest fashion for evening head-dresses consists of a single tuft of flowers combined with peacocks' feathers, but without the admixture of foliage. The tuft is won on one side of the head. Tufts of the same flowers and feathers as those in the coiffure are employed in ornamenting various parts of the dress.

The new mode of mounting field flowers, which are most in vogue at this moment, is remarkably graceful and true to nature. They present long strings negligently tied as if just put together in the field; some a mixture of poppies and wheat-ears; others of poppies, wheat-ears, and blue-bottles; others again are combinations of daisies and wheat-ears, or poppies and daisies.

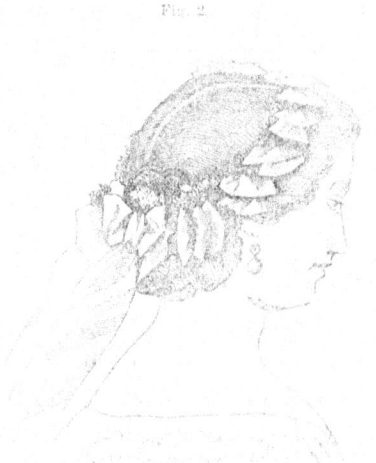

Fig. 1.—As appropriate to our exquisite fashion plate for the month, we give a decided novelty—*coiffure for a bridesmaid.* Hair banded closely, a handsome ivory or silver comb, a bandeau composed of a ruche of double crape, with bouquets of pansies, and a short illusion veil, arranged as a *câche peigné*, and flowing gracefully down over the neck.

Fig.2.—Headdress for a bridesmaid at a reception or wedding party ; a wreath of ribbon loops, blue, pink, or rose sublime, with black lace between, terminated by a flat bow, with floating ends.

COIFFURE COMPOSED OF PIECES OF BIAS SILK CUT OUT AND BOX-PLAITED.

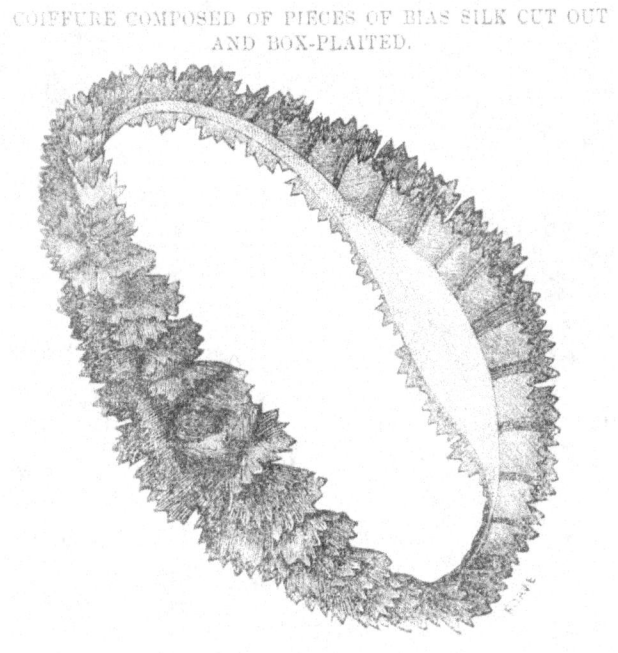

GENERAL REMARKS.—HEAD-DRESSES for ordinary wear still continue to be made of ruched silk, which is finished off, sometimes, by a row of ruched silk, which is finished off, sometimes, by a row of lace ; for the cache-peigne behind, a fanchon, or bows, or rosettes are used. The following are a few of the many which we have noticed :

A wreath of silk bows, coming rather forward in front, and finished off behind by black and colored bows. This head-dress may be made in any color, and ought to match the dress with which it is worn.

Another, a diadem of black and lilac silk rosettes, placed alternately on a ribbon foundation, with a large lilac bow at the back.

Another, composed of black and white rosettes, mixed with yellow roses.

All these head-dresses should be made rather pointed in front.

Feathers are as much worn as flowers for evening coiffures, unless for very young people, when the latter are preferable ; feathers being more suitable for older persons. Wreaths are made high in the front, diadem shape, with few flowers at the side, and a full bunch at the back forming a cache-peigne behind. Feathers are mounted on black or colored velvet coronets, trimmed with gold ornaments or velvet bows, etc. Gold combs have also become exceedingly fashionable for evening toilets.

GODEY'S LADY'S BOOK
JANUARY 1862

Fig. 3.

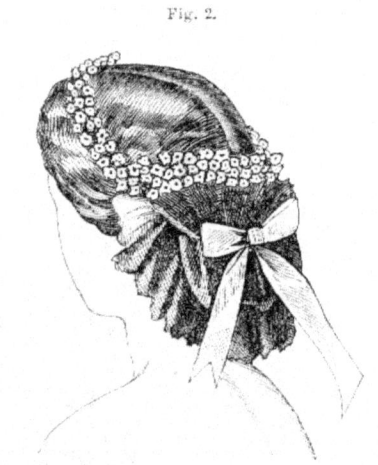

Fig. 2.

Fig. 3.—Headdress for home wear (see Chat); The bows may be of black velvet, or any suitable ribbon ; sometimes two colors are used, as magenta and black, dark blue and black.

Fig. 2—Coiffure for evening. A flat wreath of deep red English daisies, with a *caché peigné* of cherry velvet, suitable for persons having thin hair, and wearing it chiefly in front.

HEADDRESS.

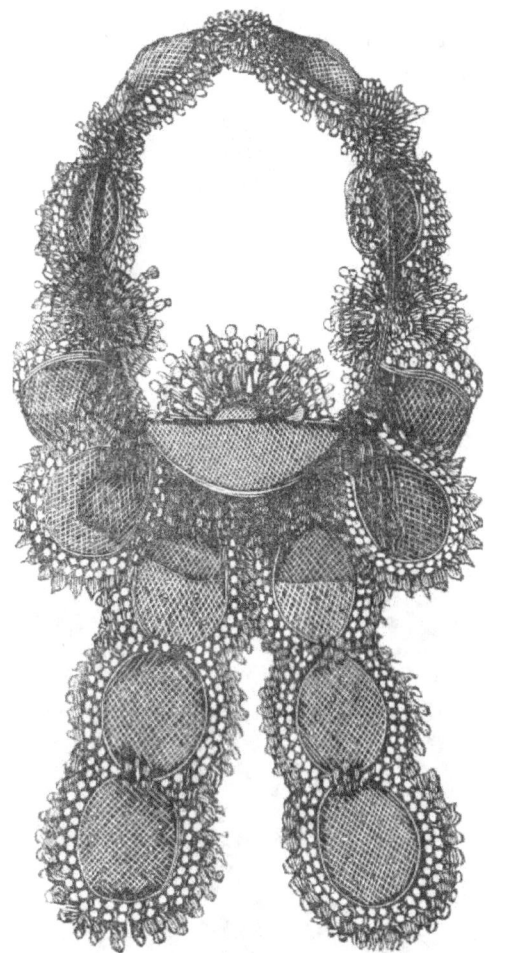

This little headdress is very simple and very easily made. It is composed of two black lace lappets and six rosettes, the rosettes having in the centre of each a small gold star or ornament. Take a piece of wire, twenty four inches long bend it in the form shown in the illustration, and fasten a piece of coarse stiff black net at the back, on which to arrange the bows and rosettes. Take the half of one of the lappets, fasten it on the wire in the middle of the front, and catch it down to the wire at intervals of three and a half inches, making the remainder of the lappet into a bow, with a short end falling on each side. The other lappet is then looped at the back, having two long ends falling in the centre; a large rosette is placed in the middle of the headdress behind, with rosettes of graduated sizes fastened to the wire where the lappets are caught down. The rosette in the middle is small, the two next rather larger, and the two at the sides larger still. For variety the lace could be ornamented with gold stars, etc.

**PETERSON'S MAGAZINE
JANUARY 1862**

HEAD-DRESS.

GENERAL REMARKS.—HEAD-DRESSES.—a stylish and elegant head-dress is formed of a diadem of black velvet, worked with stars in steel and jet. At the right side a small black feather and a bunch of roses, and a long white feather reaching round the other part of the head-dress.

A most stylish head-dress is formed Vesuve chrysanthemums, with clusters of black fruit. It is slightly raised in front, and terminated in a point at the back.

Steel and Jet are much employed in ornamenting coiffures.

GODEY'S LADY'S BOOK
MARCH 1862

Fig. 1.

Fig. 2.

Fig. 1.— A headdress rather than a cap, may be worn by a person still younger any one who desires to conceal, as much as possible thinness or loss of hair. It is made with bandeau of black velvet ribbon, which has a flat bow edged with blonde over the forehead. At the side a blush rose with pendent bud and foliage. The *câche peigné* is of blonde with loops of velvet ribbon.

Fig. 2. is of black lace roses without foliage, and black velvet ribbon. It is pointed in front.

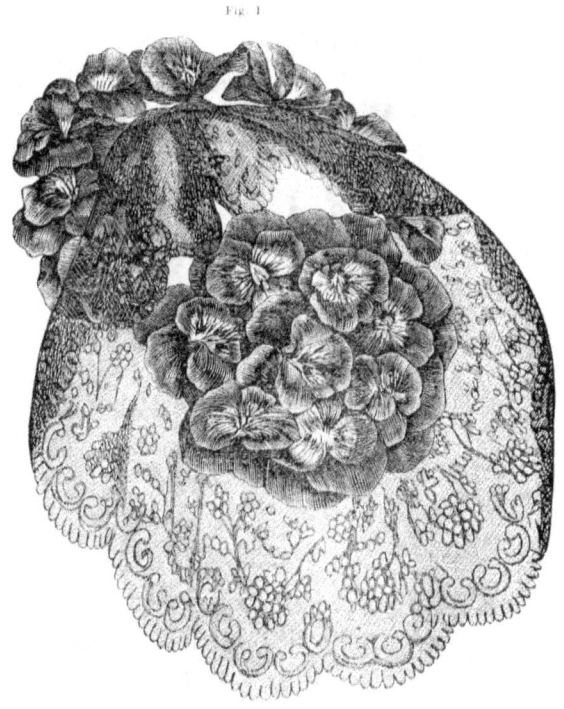

COIFFURES.

Fig. 1.—Coiffure composed of pansies and black lace.

Fig. 2.—This coiffure is very simple, and generally becoming. The rosettes are formed of pieces of bias silk, about an inch and a half in width ; the edges are cut out in points and the silk box plaited and formed into a rosette, then sewed on to stiff net ; the band can be of velvet or silk, and a bow of ribbon to match the silk is often placed on one side of the band. One or more colors can be used ; rose sublime and black make a good contrast.

Fig. 1.

Fig. 2.

Fig. 1.—Headdress for dinner or evening. *Fauchon* of black lace relieved by a ruche of blonde around the face. Bow of fuchsia col-ored-ribbon on the top ; single fuchsias in vel-vet, with leaves drooping at the side.

Fig. 2.—Headdress for opera or concert. Front hair in close rolls or puffs ; the back hair brought down very smoothly to the neck, where it is arranged in a series of close rolls. The headdress is a cordon of mauve and black velvet, twisted together ; a knot of short mauve plumes, with a star like ornament in the centre, is placed directly on the top of the head

GODEY'S LADY'S BOOK
JUNE 1862

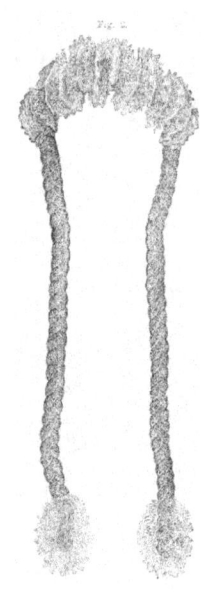

Fig. 2.— *The Valois Headdress.*— This con-sists of thick black velvet plaits, which are fas-tened at the back of the head, and the coronet is formed of standing loops of cherry velvet and black lace.

der row pink, and both colors are put on in full box-plaits. The strings at the back of the head are of black and the bows of pink ribbon. The knot of hair is to pass between the upper and lower bow, and must, consequently, be dressed quite low on the neck. Head-dresses of this description will be exceedingly fashionable this summer; their comparative cheapness, yet beauty, recommending them as especially suitable. We shall give another pattern in a different style in our next number; for different descriptions of head-dresses are required for different persons.

FIG. VII.—HEAD-DRESS OF BLACK AND PURPLE RIBBON.

The Nerissa Head-dress, an engraving of which we give above, is composed of black and pink ribbon. This head-dress is made on a band of millinette cut to fit the head, and which is stiffened with cap wire.

The upper row of ribbon is black and the un-

Fig. 1.—Coronet of black velvet, trimmed with leaves of the same material, intermixed with gold. A white ostrich feather is placed on one side of the headdress, and a bow of velvet, with ends of an unequal length. And fringed with gold, on the other side.

Fig. 2.—Coronet of plaited velvet, edged with gold braid, and having a star quite in the centre ; the loops behind should also be made of plaited velvet, edged in the same manner, but not made in such profusion as our illustration shows. Seven long loops for the bottom row, and five for the top one, would be quite sufficient ; the plaited velvet being wider, would, consequently, not require so many bows.

PETERSON'S MAGAZINE
JULY 1862

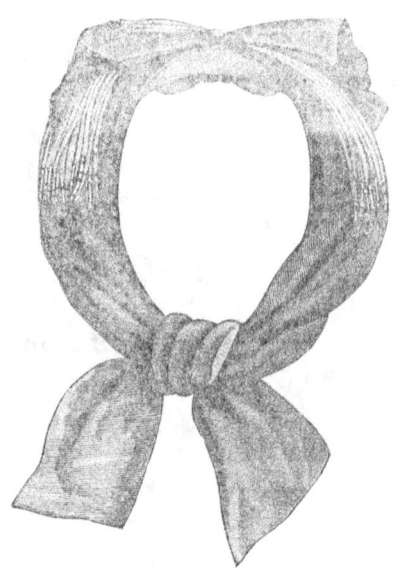

ESMERALDA HEAD-DRESS.
BY MRS. JANE WEAVER.

This beautiful head dress is composed of a roll of black velvet on a foundation of milinette, stiffened with cap wire to keep it in place. On the front of the forehead are velvet loops with long gilt pendants. A knot of velvet confines the roll at the back of the head. This head dress is beautiful in black or scarlet velvet with gold pendants, or in scarlet with black jet. We have seen one exactly like the accompanying, composed of a shade blue velvet, with the ornaments in gold wheat-ears.

THE ALCESTE HEADDRESS.
COMPOSED OF LOBELIA BLUE VELVET, WHITE BLONDE, AND A WHITE PLUME.

CHITCHAT UPON NEW YORK AND PHILADELPHIA FASHIONS FOR AUGUST.

For young ladies, there are a great many beautiful headdresses, all however encircling the head. Among the prettiest was a coronet headdress, composed of a torsade of black velvet with a white edge. A little to the left, near the top, there was a bow with a bunch of rosebuds in the centre; behind rather to the right, another and larger bow with long velvet streamers. Another was a *chicoré* ruche of black lace, rounded to form a kind of coronet, with a lace bow on the forehead, three tufts of Vesuve velvet on the right side, and a black lace barbe, forming a bow behind. A more stylish headdress was a Wreath of black velvet, twisted in with a gold cord, the wreath being square in front, and having loops of velvet blended with gold wheat-ears hanging down on the left side. Another black velvet coiffure was decorated with steel triangles and chains ; another very stylish one was composed of a diadem of black velvet, worked with stars in gold and jet, and at the back three rosettes of black velvet edged with gold, and in the centre of each a red daisy, with jet heart. A very simple headdress was a plait of scarlet velvet, with a very beautiful black and gold butterfly placed on the centre of the forehead. Another was of black velvet mixed with old oak leaves and branches of fruit.

CHITCHAT UPON NEW YORK AND PHILA-
DELPHIA FASHIONS FOR SEPTEMBER.

Nothing very new has yet appeared in the way of headdresses, with the exception of wreaths formed of loops of ribbon and flower wreaths. As it is seldom anything of this kind is suitable for mourning, we will mention several which have appeared. One was composed of two rows of white roses, with steel buttons between them, and velvet foliage ; another consisted of black hortensias and violet heartsease ; another of small white china asters with steel hearts, forming a coronet, and at the side was a branch of black willow ; another was of violet, relieved by spikes of jet.

Combs are small, and the patterns with graduated balls on the top are generally favorites . The most expensive ones are of a golden-color shell resembling amber.

GODEY'S LADY'S BOOK
OCTOBER 1862

Figs. 1 and 2 (front and back view). The Almira Headdress.

PETERSON'S MAGAZINE
OCTOBER 1862

GENERAL REMARKS.—HEAD-DRESSES are, to a certain extent, disappearing unless for *full evening toilet*, and combs, secured in plaits behind, seem to have taken their place. These combs are now made in such variety that no lady will have any difficulty in getting one to suit the color of her hair. Combs, with tortoise shell knobs, and elaborate steel, gilt, and silver tops, are amongst the most fashionable kinds; and these tops are now made with a hinge on one side, so that they may be pressed closely against the plait, or stand out a little, whichever the wearer may prefer.

Next is a bridal veil showing the manner of dressing the back hair, etc.

GODEY'S LADY'S BOOK
JANUARY 1863

HEADDRESSES.
(See description, Fashion department.)

HEADDRESSES.

Fig. 1. The Coralio Headdress.—This headdress is formed of a torsade of cerise velvet and a point lace barbe, with a large bow on the forehead, and white plumes on the right side.

Fig. 2. The Etdalio.—Net composed of gold cord caught with black velvet and gold buttons. Three white plumes are on the left side. Over the head is a roll of black velvet, which is finished on the right side by a large bow with ends trimmed with gold and lace.

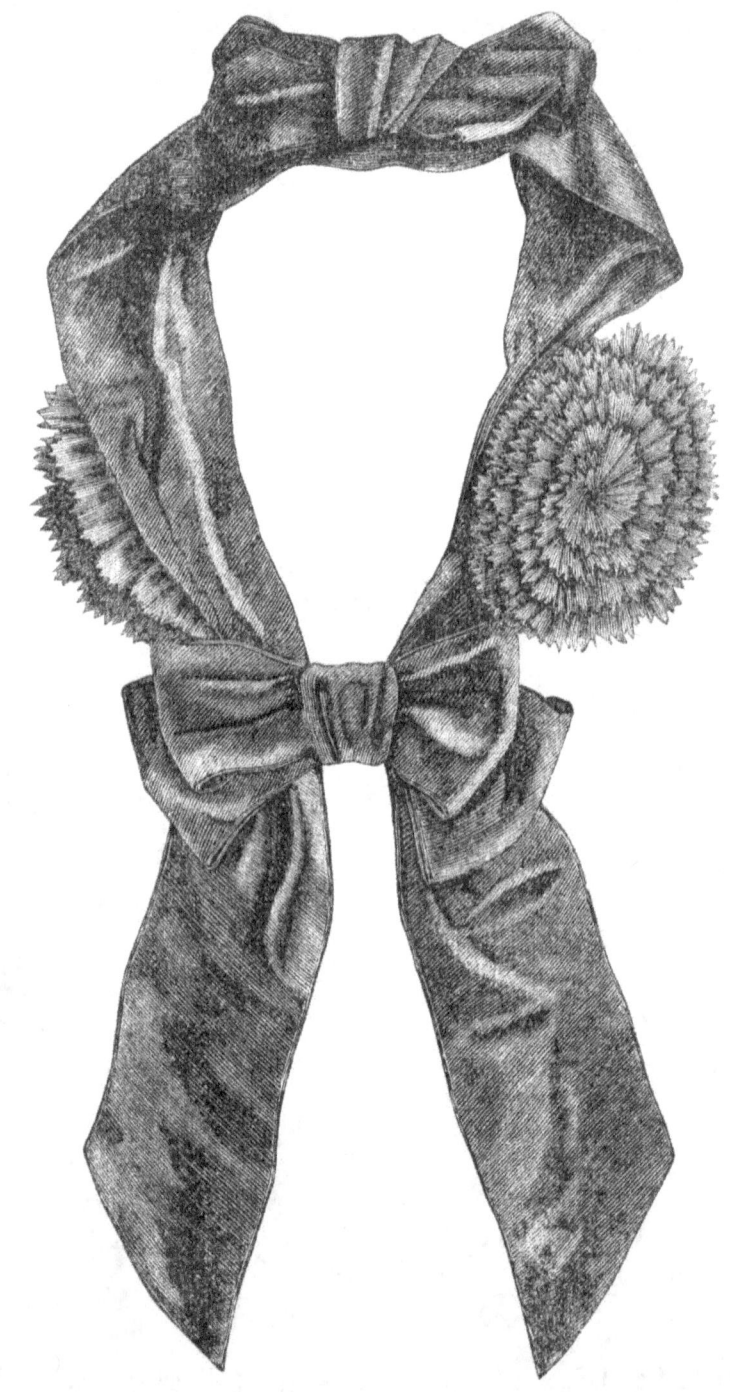

THE ESMERALDA
MADE OF BLACK AND VESUVE RIBBONS. SUITABLE FOR A
BRUNETTE.

NEW STYLES OF HEAD-DRESSES.

GENERAL REMARKS—HAIR NETS, to a certain extent, still continue to be worn under the pretty fashionable hats ; in fact, they are almost a necessity out-of-doors, if the hair is to be kept neat and tidy. The newest and most uncommon nets are those made of velvet, laced in and out, and secured to keep the squares in their proper shape, by sewing the velvet together wherever it crosses. Sometimes the velvet of which these headdresses are made is bordered on each side by a tiny white, maize, or colored edge ; and frequently a broad open fancy braid, manufactured for the purpose, is issued for these coiffures. They are usually finished off at the top with a bow of velvet, or with a coronet of plaited velvet, or a thick quilled silk ruche.

LARGE WREATHS are but seldom worn now for evening coiffure ; if flowers are used at all, they are dotted here and there about the hair (which should be very much frizzed) in tiny bunches. This style of head-dress is at once simple and becoming.

Fig. 1.

A NEW VELVET COIFFURE.

Fig. 1 represents this beautiful and simple headdress complete.

Fig. 2 is the foundation of it.

Fig. 3 shows how the velvet should be plaited, and by matching the numbers on Figs. 2 and 3, the coiffure will be arranged as in the complete plate.

The diadem plait is of three strands of velvet.

Fig. 3.

FANCY HEADDRESS.

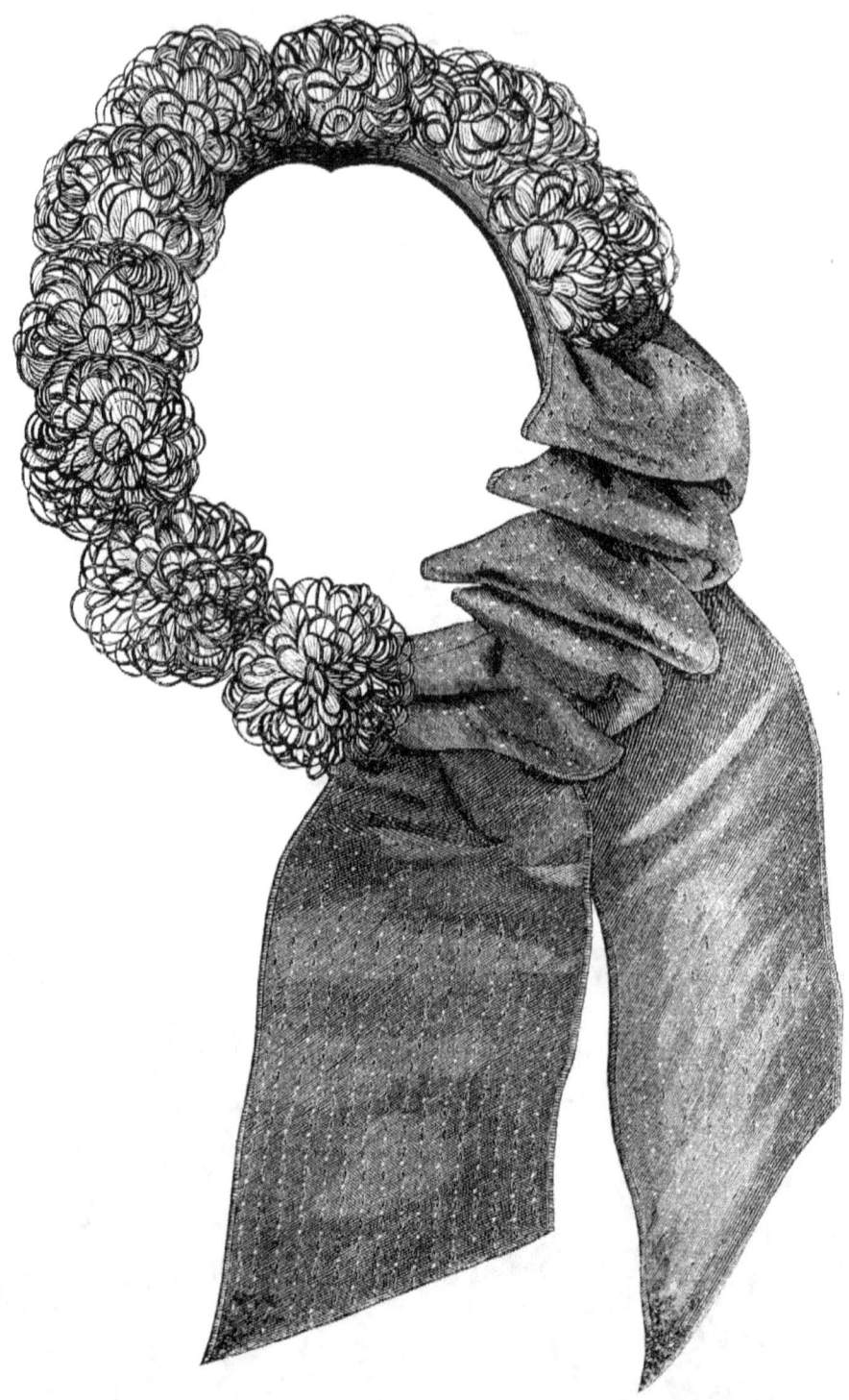

Formed of rosettes of very narrow ribbon, and loops of wide ribbon.

GENERAL REMARKS.—HEAD-DRESS.—A simple, and at the same time a most becoming wreath for the fair hair, is composed of daisies of two different shades of mauve-color. A wreath, effective with hair of any color, may be composed of small roses, separated by tufts of forget-me-nots or violets. A combination of moss-roses and myosotes also forms a charming wreath, especially for a young lady. On dark hair decided colors are most effective, and for a lady with dark complexion nothing is more becoming that a wreath of scarlet geranium, with its beautiful shaded foliage.

GODEY'S LADY'S BOOK
MARCH 1863

THE NINA HEADDRESS.

(Front view.)   (Back view.)

CHITCHAT UPON NEW YORK AND PHILADELPHIA FASHIONS FOR MARCH.

Headdresses are worn higher than ever in front. Bunches of ribbon or velvet, the size of two bands clasped together, are placed directly in front, and the larger they are, the handsomer they are considered. Others have a bunch of feathers or flowers over the forehead, and a scarf carried straight over the side of the head and from thence falls on the neck. Small wreaths are also worn on the side of the bead.

For home wear, lace barbes are arranged with a loop, and end over the plait or roll at the side of the bead, and carried over or below the back hair to the opposite side of the head, where they are pinned in a larger bow, and end just behind the ear. Black lace bows with stiff linings are also worn in front between the bandeaux, and when lined with white, are very effective.

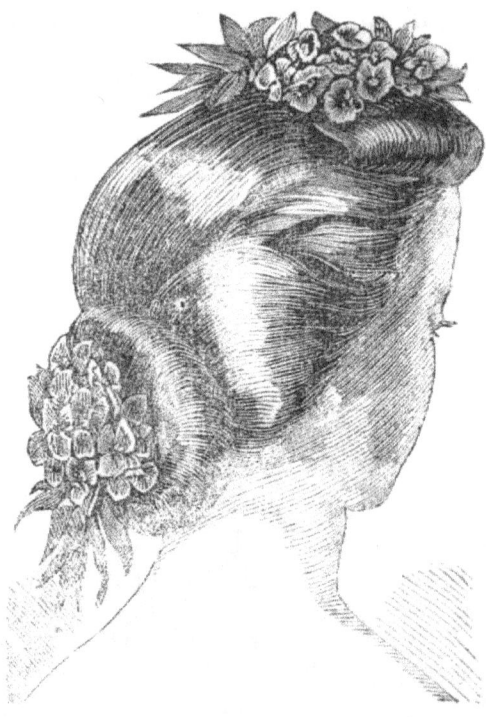

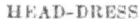

HEAD-DRESS.

HEAD-DRESS.

GENERAL REMARKS.—HEAD-DRESSES differ widely from the heavy wreaths lately worn. A puff of white tulle, a bunch of moss-roses, a branch of foliage, with the hair curled or creped between, arranged to suit the style of face, is now the most fashionable style. Birds'-nests, humming-birds, butterflies, and dragon flies are all called into requisition to form this irregular, fanciful head-gear.

GODEY'S LADY'S BOOK
APRIL 1863

CHITCHAT UPON NEW YORK AND PHILADELPHIA FOR APRIL.

We cannot close without saying a few words about the exquisite creations at Mme. Tilman's, 148 east Ninth Street, late 712 Broadway. Among the beautiful flowers, perfect gems of art, so perfect indeed that one bends down almost involuntarily to catch their fragrance, we see humming-birds, butterflies, and all kinds of brilliant winged insects lighting or seemingly flitting among the beautiful exotics. The birds and butterflies are of course perfect, being the teal birds and insects preserved and mounted. The flowers are all arranged in the coronet form, some merely the coronet mounted on a wire, or band of velvet, others with a spray or tuft of flowers directly at the back ; while another style which pleased us greatly, both for its simplicity and its exact representation of nature, had a spray and stem of the white locust, forming a coronet, and at the side was another spray of the same pattern falling gracefully over the neck.

THE LATEST PARISIAN STYLES FOR HEADDRESSES, ETC.

(See description, Fashion department.)

HEADDRESSES, ETC.

Fig. 1.—A coiffure for the back of the head. It Is formed of very rich and wide black ribbon, with moss-roses, buds, and foliage.

Fig. 2.—A coiffure in the coronet style. It can be made of any color to suit the complexion of the wearer. We would suggest, as very stylish, the roll and front puffed loops to be of a rich garnet ribbon, with gold ornament and short white plumes.

Fig. 3.— A ball coiffure, composed of green ribbon and a large tuft of roses with foliage.

Fig. 4.—One of the newest ball coiffures. Branches of wood twined together, with a large tuft of Narcissus blossoms, with long, graceful leaves, forming a coronet. A smaller tuft of flowers rests on the neck at the back.

Fig. 5.—Coiffure for full ball dress. A scarlet peony forming the coronet, and at the sides sprigs of ivy, oak leaves, and gold acorns on branches of wood.

Fig. 6.—A wreath formed of white lilies, violet hyacinths, and Vesuve ribbons, twined gracefully round the wood branches. This is also in the coronet style, and being of moderate height it is exceedingly pretty and becoming.

HEAD-DRESS.

GODEY'S LADY'S BOOK
JUNE 1863

NEW COIFFURES.

NEW COIFFURES.

Fig. 1.—This coiffure is composed of puffed ribbon and bows mounted on a wire, with flowers at the side and a lace barbe looped behind and fastened with ornamental pins. The color of the ribbon should correspond with the dress with which it is worn, or should form a decided contrast.

Fig. 2.—The hair is dressed with three rolls on each side of the face. The wreath is made very full in front, and has a gold cord and tassel trimmed in with it. It gradually diminishes in size towards the back, small bands forming pendants behind.

Fig. 4.—Coiffure of the latest style.

Fig. 5.—Fancy coiffure, formed of a scarf of black lace and bouquets of flowers. The large tuft of flowers is placed over the forehead, and the scarf is laid rather on the side of the head, and finished very low on the neck with a small tuft of flowers. This is one of the newest and most stylish headdresses. Velvet and cashmere scarfs are often substituted for the black lace.

CHITCHAT UPON NEW YORK AND PHILADEL-
PHIA FASHIONS FOR JUNE.

A pretty novelty appeared, in the wreaths intended for the six bridesmaids. They were each of the simplest flowers, lightly mounted with grass in bloom, and each wreath a different flower. Buttercups, wild roses, the downy white tops of the dandelions, with blades of grass spangled with dew, violets, and Gnelder roses, made up this novel and charming set of decorations for one of the most fashionable weddings that the daily prints have chronicled this " season of flowers."

FANCY COIFFURES.—(*See description, Fashion department.*)

Fig. 1.

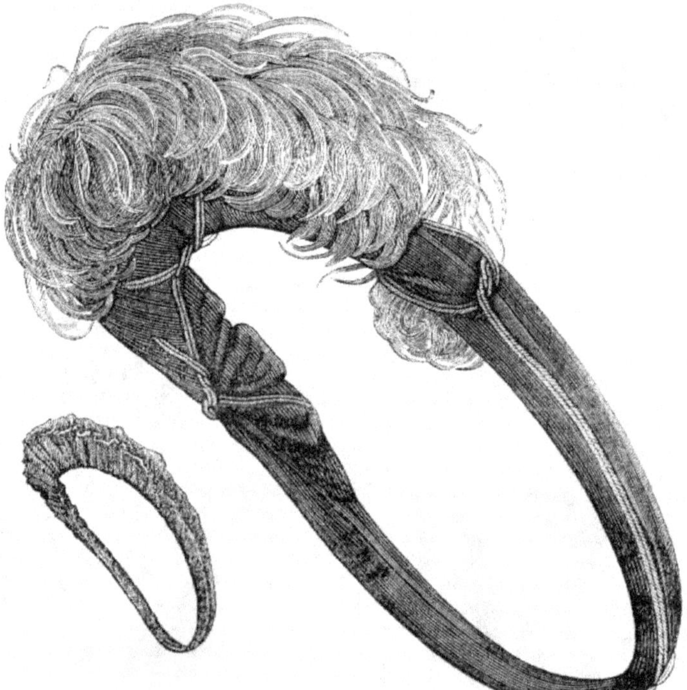

Fig. 2.

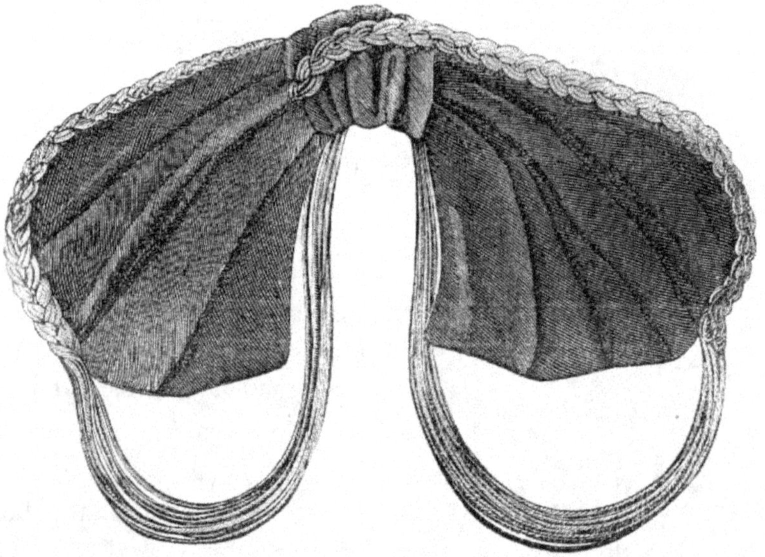

FANCY COIFFURES.

Fig. 1.—A fancy coiffure, made of ruby velvet, gold cord, and a white plume. The small cut refers to the coiffure without the plume. This is one of the most desirable styles.

Fig. 2.—Butterfly coiffure, suitable for a young lady. It is for the back of the head, and made of black velvet and gold cord.

HEADDRESS.

Hair turned off the face, and both back and front arranged very loosely over frizettes. The wreath is composed of large pink roses, with their buds and foliage also fancy grasses.

PETERSON'S MANGAZINE
JULY 1863

GENERAL REMARKS.—HEAD-DRESSES remain as they were worn during the past winter ; they are high in front with a cluster of flowers, plain at the sides, and ornamented again at the back. This style proves more becoming than the formal wreath, and each separate head can be arranged to suit its particular style ; and as no two heads or faces are alike, this is a more rational proceeding than when both oval, round, and square faces appeal alike with formal wreaths round them.

LATEST PARISIAN STYLES OF HEADDRESSES, ETC.

(See description, Fashion department.)

HEADDRESSES, ETC.

Fig. 1.—Coiffure of black velvet and black lace, with A coronet of roses, on which is a small humming-bird.

Fig. 2.—Coiffure formed of black lace and black ribbon, flowers, and a cluster of cherries.

Fig 3.— Headdress of scarlet velvet edged with black lace, having a coronet of flowers and loops of velvet mingled with lace.

Fig. 4.—Black velvet coiffure, with gold ornaments and scarlet flowers.

Fig. 5—A thick roll of brown velvet, with heavy coronet of roses and light flowers.

Fig. 6.—A very stylish coiffure composed of Magenta velvet and gold ornaments, with a tuft of white flowers on the left side.

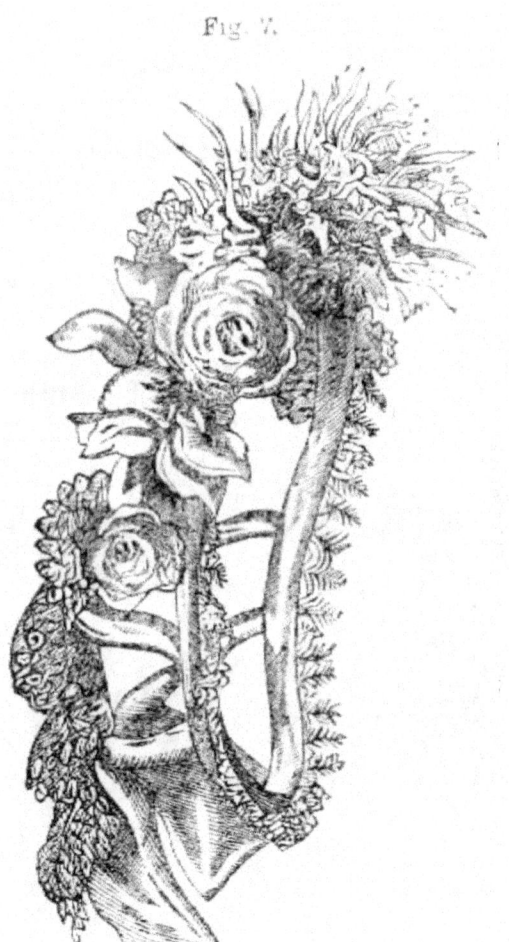

Fig. 7.

Fig. 7.—Coiffure composed of lavender velvet and black lace, and highly ornamented with roses and fancy grasses.

CHITCHAT UPON NEW YORK AND PHILADELPHIA FASHIONS FOR AUGUST.

The prettiest coiffure for this dress, is La Gitana, which particularly attracted our attention at Mme. Tilman's, of 143 East Ninth Street, New York. It was the most fascinating combination of gleaming scarlet verbenas, enameled leaves, grass, and scarlet ribbon bordered with black, falling in long graceful pendants. Imagine a rich brunette complexion and sparkling black eyes, beneath this fanciful coquetry.

The Coiffure Caliste.
(Front and back view)
This headdress is composed of bandeaux bouffants at each side of the head, and a full bow fixed low at the back. A wreath of red verbena passes along one side, the flowers being disposed in a full cluster in front of the forehead, and forming a *câche-peigne* at the back of the head.

Fig. 7.

Fig. 7.—Coiffure, made of black illusion, cherry velvet ribbon, and cherry flowers. Suitable for a young married lady for dinner or evening dress.

GENERAL REMARKS.—HEAD-DRESSES are worn rather lower in front than formerly, and the Marie Stuart form of cap is much sought after by those ladies who wear their hair either waved or in short ringlets. A very pretty head-dress is composed of cerise velvet ribbon, edged on each side with black lace; this is carried across the forehead with some buds of the cactus plant, intermingled with black lace leaves; while upon the back hair rests a cactus in full bloom. A headdress composed of a half-handkerchief of black lace, with a bouquet of field flowers, and a ruche of plaid ribbon, has also had much success. Young ladies wear nets made of purple silk, with a coronet of purple crepe lisse round their heads; these are very becoming to dark and pale complexions, but for fair ones the same style is produced in sky-blue and lilac.

GODEY'S LADY'S BOOK
OCTOBER 1863

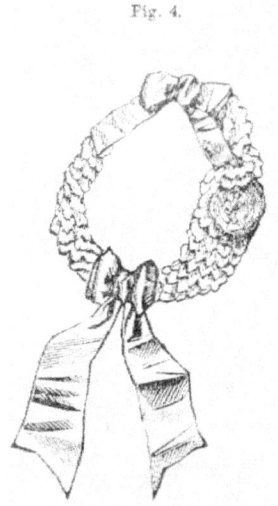

Fig. 4.

Fig. 4.—Headdress, composed of lace and rose sublime ribbon.

CHITCHAT UPON NEW YORK AND PHILADELPHIA FASHIONS FOR OCTOBER.

There is nothing new in the form of head-dresses. The two most popular styles are the coronet and the spray of flowers at the side of the head. All flowers are now mounted on gutta percha, which gives the appearance of natural stems, and makes them more pliable than the old-fashioned wire mountings. Bows of ribbon, velvet, and lace are frequently substituted for the spray of flowers. This style, we may say, is universal, and adopted both by young and married ladies.

Many of our belles are weaving natural flowers among their tresses. It is a Spanish fashion, and very beautiful. Still natural blossoms are so frail that, unless constantly renewed, but few will retain their freshness during an evening. We think, therefore, we prefer the imitations of nature, as they can scarcely be detected from the originals, and are decidedly more economical. We learn from our Paris correspondent that a noted French artificial florist has introduced small oranges into bridal wreaths, to overcome the heavy effect of the orange blossoms and buds only ; green, it is said, not being admissible in bridal wreaths. We have as yet seen nothing of the kind ; therefore, cannot recommend them. Indeed we do not like the idea at all. We think nothing can be prettier than orange blossoms with their rich glossy green leaves mingled with sprays of the pure and graceful lily of the valley. Green must necessarily be introduced into a bridal wreath to relieve the white; other wise it is exceedingly tame. Daisies are being substituted in Paris for the lilies ; but we consider pendant flowers the more graceful. The back hair is generally arranged in a waterfall, frequently tied with a bright ribbon or velvet. Bunches of braids are also caught up in the same style.

THE PSYCHE BUTTERFLY FOR HEADDRESSES.

(See description, Work department.)

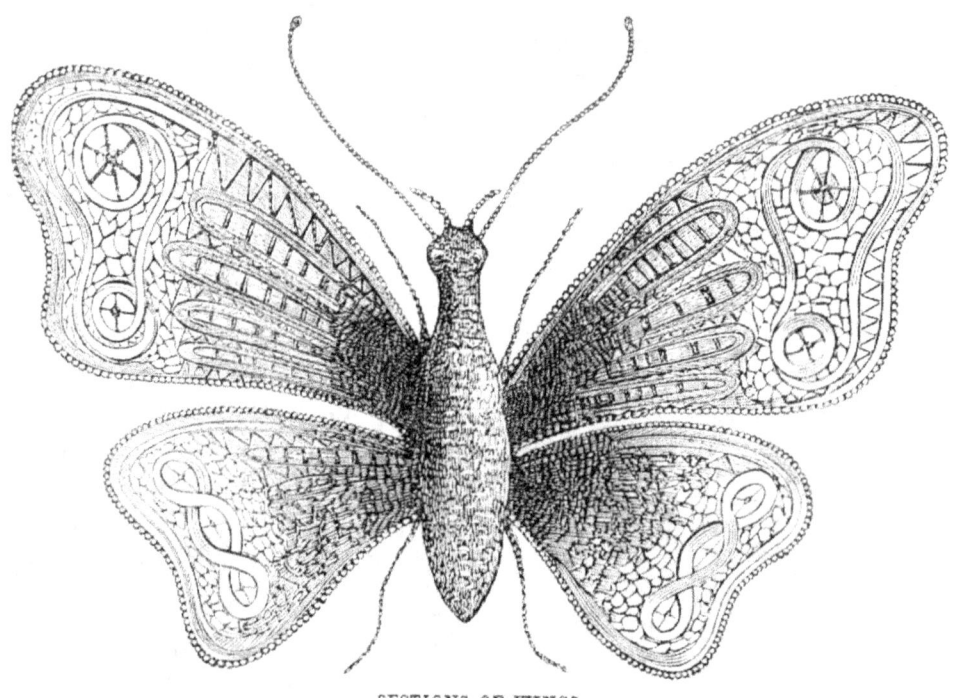

SECTIONS OF WINGS.

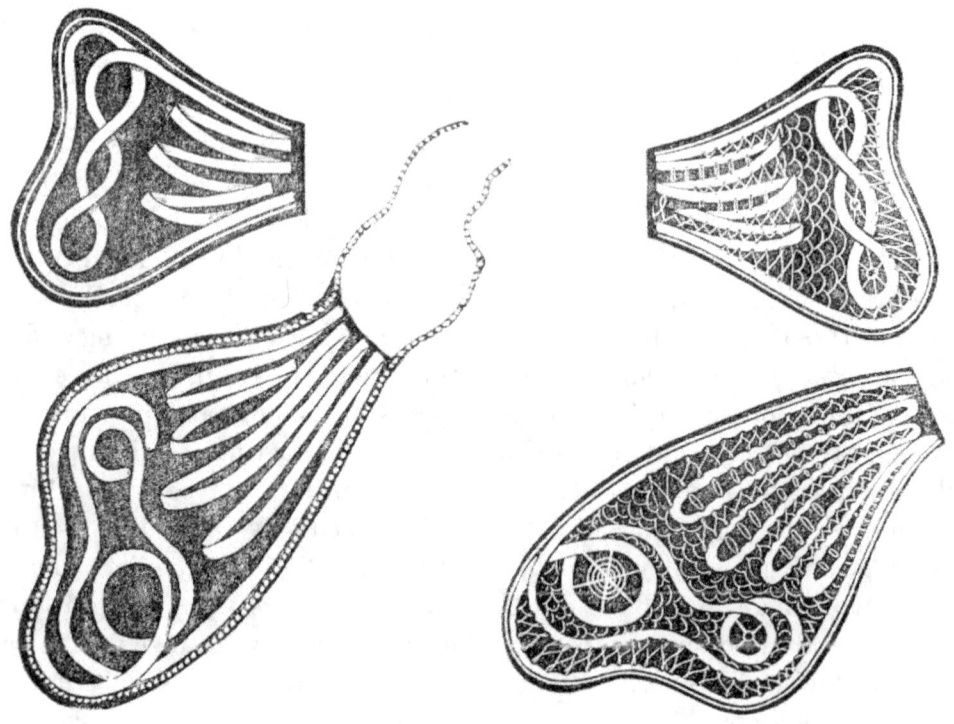

THE PSYCHE BUTTERFLY.

Materials. — Three yards of narrow gold braid, a skein of fine gold twine, one yard of gold spiral wire, and a skein each of white, light blue, and cerise fine silk. This elegant ornament is now much used in ball-room costume, either as a headdress, when it is attached to the hair in the centre of the forehead, or on the left side of the head nearly at the back ; it is also placed on the skirt of the dress to loop up the tunic or drapery, and it may be applied to a variety of articles, as pen-wipers, paper weights, screens, etc.

The sections of the wings are given, one showing the braid outline only, and the other the stitches, which are worked to attach the braids together. The wings and body are made separately, the latter being formed of plain crochet.

Commence by tracing the braid outline of one of the sections, and with a fine sewing-needle and thread tack the gold braid on the outline. These stitches should be taken across the braid, and not through it ; then, with the blue silk and a sewing-needle, begin at the narrow part of the wing, and run the silk across the braids, darning it in and out of them eight or ten times ; then work up the braids, joining them with rows of hem-stitch. The network above them is of the cerise silk, and formed of a succession of open button-hole stitches.

The rosettes in the centre of the circles are made of white silk, and to form them see the braid pattern in the preceding direction ; the space between the two straight lines at the edge should be filled with blue silk. When the work is finished, sew the gold wire round the edge of the braid, using the cerise silk, and at each side leave about two inches of the wire to form the legs. Commence now on the body.

The Body.—Work with the gold twine and Penelope crochet needle, No. 3. Commence with 4 chain stitches, and work a single stitch in the first chain to make it round. Work 2 plain stitches in each of the 4 stitches, then 2 plain both in one stitch, and 3 plain in successive stitches, 8 times ; it will now be 16 stitches round. Work 80 plain; stuff the work with a little piece of wool. Decrease by taking two stitches together and working them as one stitch ; then 5 plain, and decrease again, 8 times ; and for the head, work 2 stitches in 1, 5 times ; then 6 plain ; and for the antennae, take 3 inches of the gold wire, and, leaving half of it in front, place it along the last round, and work it under for 3 plain stitches. Leave the other end in the front, work 4 plain, then 4 single, take 2 together 5 times, miss 1, and 1 single, 3 times ; then 3 chain, miss 1, and 2 single on it ; 3 chain again, miss 1, and 2 single on it, 1 single on the head, and fasten off. Sew two beads above the antennae for the eyes ; then sew the wings to the sides of the body, leaving the wire for the legs.

COIFFURE HORTENSE.

CHITCHAT UPON NEW YORK AND PHILADEL-
PHIA FASHIONS FOR DECEMBER.

The ball coiffures were veritable Parisian in-
spirations. One, La Gloire, was of olive leaves
meeting in a high point in front, with wide
gold braid twined through it with unstudied
grace.

Most of the wreaths were of the coronet

style, with long trains or sprays, three-quarters of a yard long, on each side. These could be left to hang or caught up in the hair. Bridal coiffures were of this style. Another pretty wreath was a coronet of strawberries with foliage, branches of wood twisted at the side, and a bunch of berries at the back.

A most charming and novel style of head-dress was formed of linked chains of scarlet velvet, caught in with flowers. Some of the pendants had anchors attached, and the whole was original and stylish. With these head-dresses, the velvet combs to match should be worn. These are another pretty novelty for the winter. We were shown a variety of velvet headdresses, studded with jeweled stars, flowers, bugs, crescents, and exquisite butterflies. These jeweled ornaments are very effective, and will be in great demand this winter.

The good taste of the Parisian modiste in everything relating to head gear is an undisputed fact, and in this graceful art Mme. Tilman has no rival, certainly on this side of the water.

PETERSON'S MAGAZINE
DECEMBER 1863

HEAD-DRESS OF FLOWERS AND LACE.

HEAD-DRESS.

GENERAL REMARKS.—THE HEAD-DRESSES are particularly effective and pretty ; they are simple and yet tasteful. The field and wild flowers, which for the last three months have been worn upon bonnets and hats, are now popular upon simple head-dresses. A black ribbon is twisted carelessly yet gracefully round the head, and upon the top a bouquet of scarlet poppies and oats placed; a black lace lappet mingles with the flowers and hangs down at the back. Water-lilies, geraniums, clematis, and mauve-colored roses are also frequently formed into tasteful head-dress with black lace; sometimes what the French call a *herisson* of blonde is added to the flowers. We should smile were we to translate literally, and to speak of a hedgehog of blonde in English ; the simile is comical, yet nothing gives us the same idea of the bristling erect appearance the blonde should present as does that harmless little animal.

There is no new form in the wreaths which

have been fashionable during the autumn. They are still worn high and pointed in front, and are mounted upon gutta percha, which presents the appearance of natural branch. This should be twisted and entwined carelessly, so as to look as unstudied and natural as possible. The blue convolvulus, with its brilliant coloring, graceful leaves, and twining stalks and tendrils, being especially suitable to such a style of head-dress. Thick gold cord is sometimes employed for mounting flowers upon, instead of gutta percha; it is more brilliant, but not so natural-looking.

PETERSON'S MAGAZINE
JANUARY 1864

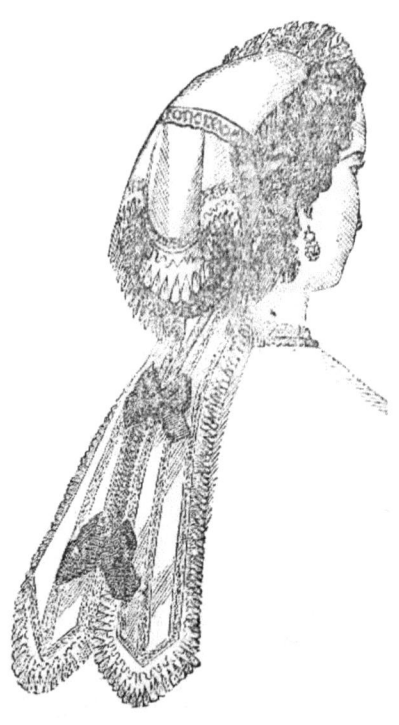

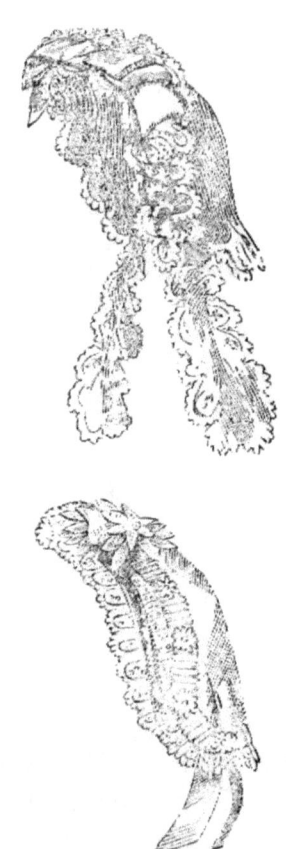

VARIETIES FOR THE MONTH.
BY EMILY H. MAY.

Our third illustration is an Italian head-dress; something entirely new, and very charming. This graceful affair has created quite a sensation with the greatest success, in the fashionable circles of Philadelphia, New York, and Boston. It has a picturesque air, as will be seen, which very few similar articles attain. On a tall, willowy form it is particularly pretty. It has a careless, artistic effect on such persons, as if handkerchief had been thrown, lightly, over the head, and the ends allowed to fall down. It is, on all persons, singularly free from the stiffness so common to so many head-dresses.

THE MIRANDA COIFFURE.

COMPOSED of scarlet velvet twined with gold cord, and the ends fringed with gold fringe. A network formed of bands of velvet forms a *cache-peigne* for the chignon.

VARIETIES FOR THE MONTH.

We give, again, some of the newest patterns in head-dresses, etc., as we did in the January number. The first to which we call attention is a charming head-dress, one of the very prettiest sent out, from Paris, this winter. The next is also a head-dress, in some respects more elaborate than the last ; and of this we give a back view.

GENERAL REMARKS.—HEAD-DRESSES OF PLAID VELVET SILK are greatly in vogue for young ladies; they are worn with two straps round the head in front, and a bow at the left side one of the straps only is carried to the back; in this there is elastic, so the headdress can be pulled forward or backward at will. Narrow self-colored ribbon velvet is also made up into headdresses; these are placed flat round the head tied underneath the left ear, and are finished off at the top of the side with a rosette.

CHITCHAT UPON NEW YORK AND PHILADELPHIA FASHION FOR MARCH.

In headdresses we saw many exquisite novelties. The coronet is still the prevailing style, but a pretty variation of it was a double wreath. The first rather more than a quarter of a yard in circumference, the other still smaller and linked in it. It was formed of an exquisite bunch of roses and buds, which was to be placed just over the forehead between the puffs, and the rest was of small buds and leaves. A large rose in the second wreath was intended to ornament the top of the waterfall coiffure.

Another headdress was of very large pansies of purple, scarlet, and blue velvet, with mother-of-pearl centres painted to resemble the originals. It was very elegant. Mother-of-pearl is the great novelty in the late head-dresses. Large aigrettes in the Scotch style formed of a very elegantly polished snail-shell, from which dart out three long feather-shaped shells, are introduced into many of the wreaths and headdresses.

A most exquisite wreath, a veritable Undine, was of water lilies, with tiny shells clinging to the leaves of flowers. Another head-dress was of pink roses and forget-me-nots, profusely sprinkled with large crystal raindrops.

The rage for birds and insects is not yet over. Indeed, it is on the increase, and reptiles are now being introduced. Every time we visit the rooms of Mme. Tilman we are shown something still more peculiar.

Among the very latest novelties are snails, large caterpillars, such as we see on grape-vines, and as long and thick as a lady's little finger, butterflies made of the most transparent materials, others of mother-of-pearl, beautifully colored, dragonflies and snakes. Yes, dear readers, actually snakes, fully a quarter of a yard long. All these reptiles so closely imitate nature that you really feel reluctant to take them up and examine them. We think this mania rather carried to excess. But what is to be done. The ladies are never satisfied, novelties must be had. Like Oliver Twist, they still ask for more.

Artificial flowers are in great demand, and are exquisitely perfect; and when arranged with the taste peculiar to Mme. Tilman, nothing can be more beautiful.

The Greek coiffure is one of the favorite styles, either a large bunch of curls thrown over a comb, or the more artistic style of a roll with the curls falling from the centre of it.

The most suitable style of headdress for this coiffure is a bandeau of velvet starred with brilliants. Another style is a small diadem advancing in a point upon the forehead, and studded with shells, crescents or other fancy ornaments. A comb should be made to match this headdress either of shells and velvet, or velvet and whatever ornaments are on the bandeau.

Fancy combs are still the rage, and very economical ones may be made by cutting a fancy design out of cardboard, such as knots, bows, linked rings, etc., and covering them with gilt, steel, or jet beads and fastening them on a small plain comb.

HEADDRESSES.

Fig.1—Headdress of white plumes, the hair rolled up to one side of the head, the ends allowed to hang in curls, the curls fastened by a jeweled ornament. The back hair rolled up and fastened by an ornamented comb, which can be seen from the front.

Fig. 2—Headdress of pink roses and leaves, arranged in a large bouquet in front ; in the back so arranged as to appear to catch the delicate lace coiffure and keep it in its place. The back hair arranged in puffs ; the upper part of the front rolled back, the under part curled and allowed to hang down.

NOVELTIES FOR APRIL

Fig. 1—A headdress of lilac velvet petunias, with groups of palm leaves ; a double chain of gutta percha is carried round the head ; in front, among the palm leaves, is an enameled blue and green golden serpent.

HEAD-DRESS.

Fig. 2—A Louis XV. Wreath, made with

Malmaison roses, buds, and foliage, tied with a green satin and black velvet bow. This head-dress is in two parts ; the large chaplet is placed upon the forehead, and the second, which is tied with ribbon, is arranged at the side.

Fig. 3.—A black velvet headdress, with gold

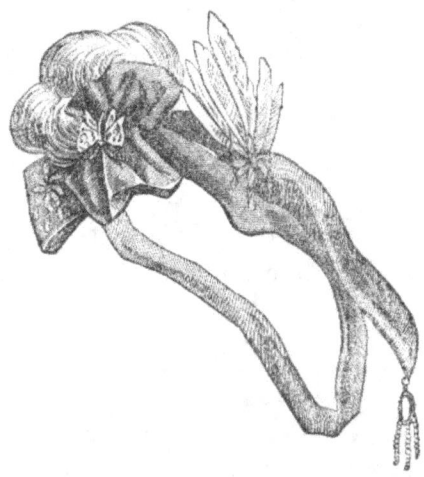

ornaments ; a mother-of-pearl butterfly at the side ; a tuft of marabout feathers spangled with mother-of-pearl in front.

Fig.4—A headdress, composed with dark red

velvet, which is formed into a large pansy in front, with a gold ornament in its centre ; a tuft of white feathers at the side.

Fig. 5.—A headdress, composed with large blue velvet pansies, with gold and mother-pearl hearts ; brown and gilt leaves.

Fig. 5.

Fig. 6.—A wreath of white forget-me-nots, with moss-roses, buds, and foliage at the side and back.

CHICHAT UPON NEW YORK AND PHILADELPHIA FASHIONS FOR APRIL

A very pretty and simple headdress for a young lady is formed of two bands of plaid velvet round the front of the head, and a large bow at the left side. One band only passes round the head, and in this is an elastic so that it may be arranged high or low to suit the coiffure. Thick gold cords are frequently entwined in the hair with good effect.

In the present number we give some very excellent headdresses, not from the *Maison Tilman*, but of their stamp. Our readers will now see how the little oddities, such as snakes and the mother of pearl butterflies, are arranged, though the cuts, we admit, give but a faint idea of the elegant originals.

Mother-of-pearl, which we first saw introduced in the Tilman headdresses, and of which we spoke in our last chat, is rapidly gaining ground. The ever-varying colors it emits by gas light render it a valuable addition to an evening toilet. The pearly part of the shell is separated in strips as thin as paper, and with these lavers, trembling oats and wheat ears are admirable well imitated. These mixed with other flowers and arranged on the head and over the dress, produce a glittering and beautiful effect.

CRAPE BUTTERFLY FOR HEAD DRESSES
BY MRS. JANE WEAVER

As it is now the fashion to use butterflies for ornamenting bonnets, and head-dresses, our readers will, perhaps, be glad to find the explanation of one. Butterflies are made more or less elegant; but this is one of the simplest and also of the cheapest kind. To form the body which the following illustration represents, half finished, twist a piece of wool fourteen round the forefinger and the middle finger ; before taking off the wool from these fingers, take a piece of wire about one inch and a half long, round which some black silk should be neatly rolled; bend it in half and place inside the wool, so that the ends may come out, as shown in the engraving. Next tie the bunch of wool, in two different places, tightly with

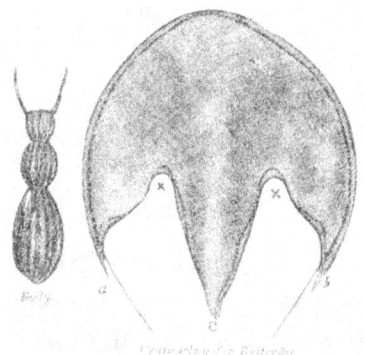

strong thread; the first time wire must be tightly fastened; this is clearly shown. Now cover the body over green crape, or with any color that may preferred.

To make the wings, you must cut out crepe in the shape shown in the illustration, and, in the outer edge, run a piece of very fine wire. Four similar wings should be cut out, to complete the butterfly.

The places marked with a cross show the place where the folds are to be made ; the points $a\ b\ c$ should be sewn together, and the wings attached to the body, as represented in the complete butterfly. Two beads are added for the eyes, and the top of the head is finished of a few stitches in black or brown silk.
(Also shown in Godey's May 1864)

GENERAL REMARKS.—HEAD-DRESSES.— For small evening parties, dinners, or opera, nets, when made with fine gold braid, are very becoming, and give additional smartness to a toilet. Many young ladies are satisfied with a large bow of either sky-blue or ponceau velvet, mixed with gold braid, fastened to the center of the net, and the head-dress is finished; others add flowers. For evening-head dresses, wide velvet plaits of some lively color have been introduced; these cover back hair only, the rest of the head remains unadorned, with the exception of a cross piece of velvet, which crosses the forehead, terminating at the side with a bouquet either pink or white roses, corn-flowers, companulas, etc., etc. The selection of the flowers depends upon the color the dress.

Another style of head-dress consists of two separate puffs of flowers joined by a rolled velvet ribbon, one to be placed above the forehead and one in the back hair. One of these was composed of white and pink narcissus, another of chrysanthemums with frosted petals and snowy leaves. The same are made in hops, with the buds in pink, blue, and various colors.

Fig. 1.   Fig. 2.

HEADDRESSES

Fig. 1.—Coiffure for a married lady. The front hair is in double rolls, and the back in three long double loops. The headdress is of point lace, roses, and fancy flowers.

Fig. 2.—Headdress of corn flowers and wheat-ears, arranged in three bouquets. The hair rolled off the face on top of head on cushions ; at the side, on puffs. The back hair arranged in waterfall style.

GODEY'S LADY'S BOOK
JUNE 1864

CHITCHAT UPON NEW YORK AND PHILADELPHIA FASHIONS FOR JUNE.

Tulle scarfs are now worn in the hair, and this soft aerial material is generally found very becoming. Bands of velvet, studded with Venetian shells and arranged as fillets, are also much worn. Half torsodes of velvet trimmed with feathers, or insects made of *burgau*, also half wreaths, are among the newest headdresses. It would probably be well to add, that the half wreath is arranged on the side of the head, and falls in one long spray over the shoulders.

The Louis 15th wreath accords so well with the present coiffures, that it is exceedingly popular. The style is for instance, a wreath of roses high in front, shallow at the sides, and directly at the back is one large rose with frosted leaves and frequently lumps of transparent ice. A long branch of buds and leaves trails on the shoulders.

CHITCHAT UPON NEW YORK AND PHILADELPHIA FASHIONS FOR JULY.

Much artistic skill is displayed in the arrangement of headdresses, though there is but little change in the style ; nor will there be, until there is a decided change in the arrangement of the hair.

Sprays of pink coral, scarcely to be detected from the real article, arranged with grasses and shells, form a charming coiffure. Marie Antoinette tufts of the rarest flowers, and of the most graceful coloring, are to be found at Mme. Tilman's. Of the tufts and half wreaths of which we have spoken in a previous article, we shall shortly give illustrations. Many other beautiful fantasies we could mention ; but we must also speak of children's hats.

PETERSON'S MAGAZINE
JULY 1864

NEW STYLE HEAD-DRESSES

GENERAL REMARKS.—HEAD-DRESSES.— The water lilies appear to be at present the favorite flowers for head-dresses for evening wear, with small helioes (those known as Venetian shells,) upon the green leaves, and the flowers themselves glistening with dew drops. Sprays of coral, with sea weeds and small shells clinging to them, are also very fashionable; likewise grasses with mother-of-pearl butterflies, and mother-of-pearl single flowers, are very popular for evening wear. Amid the grasses there are pearl, steel, and glass beads, threaded upon thin wire, which, when arranged as sprays, have a pretty light effect at candle-light.

Fig. 10.

Fig. 11.

NOVELTIES FOR AUGUST

Fig. 10.—Half wreath, composed of crimson roses, white flowers, and foliage.

Fig. 11.—A coiffure composed of scarlet velvet, spun glass, a white flower, and a gilt butterfly.

HEAD-DRESSES IN THE LATEST STYLES

GODEY'S LADY'S BOOK
SEPTEMBER 1864

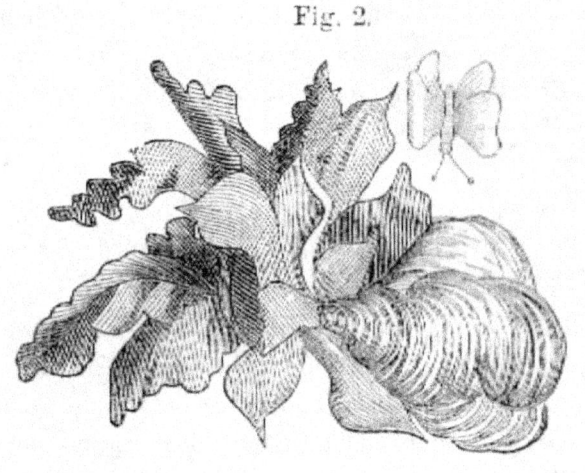

Fig. 3.—Fancy coiffure, composed of sea-green velvet, black lace, and pink roses.

Fig. 2.—A Marie Antoinette tuft, composed of light white feathers, frosted leaves, and a gilt butterfly, which is attached by a fine wire.

Fig. 11.

Fig. 14.

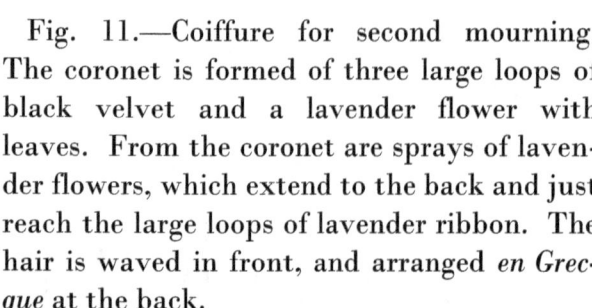

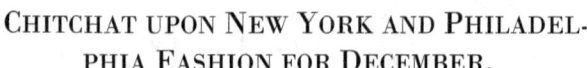

Fig. 11.—Coiffure for second mourning. The coronet is formed of three large loops of black velvet and a lavender flower with leaves. From the coronet are sprays of lavender flowers, which extend to the back and just reach the large loops of lavender ribbon. The hair is waved in front, and arranged *en Grecque* at the back.

Fig. 14.—Half wreath, composed of black velvet, roses, and white flowers.

CHITCHAT UPON NEW YORK AND PHILADELPHIA FASHION FOR DECEMBER.

The coronet style of headdress is no longer the favorite. Clusters and branches of flowers are now the adopted styles, and from the hands of Madame Tilman these are perfect types of elegance. These branches and clusters fall very low upon the shoulders and are frequently arranged very low on l ight-colored chenille with good effect. Half wreaths of mountain ash or holly-berries, dotted with white flowers, are very graceful. The beautiful wax-like camellias are quite prominent in many of the tasteful toilettes ; some are surrounded by Parma violets, and form poufs; at other times they are mounted on scarlet velvet with admirable effect.

VARIETIES FOR THE MONTH
BY EMILY H. MAY.

The autumn moths, October especially, always bring a great variety of new fashions. In the present number there is a very rich assortment of styles in dresses, capes, hats, bonnets, etc.,

The other one, with the bird in front, is particularly elegant. For this bird a butterfly

may be substituted, with equal effect. In choosing between these, and other head-dresses, ladies should always bear in mind

etc. Some of these are given in the front of the number and described in the usual department ; others we give here. The first is a head-dress, trimmed with lace and pink ribbon, a very showy and stylish affair: most of our fair readers can make it from the engraving alone. The next two are head-dresses of a different kind, after the latest made in Paris: these require a little more skill, and would be difficult to make, except for a *modiste*. The easiest to make is the first, a muslin cap, which is trimmed with lilac ribbon, on which are placed butterflies.

their style and complexion, as well as the dress they expect to wear with the head-dress. French women always think of these things. A head-dress may be very pretty in itself and yet be very unsuitable. The colors may not harmonize, or it may not suit the style of the face. A quiet tone in a costume is always the most lady-like: hence glaring colors, in a head-dress, should generally be avoided.

PETERSON'S MAGAZINE
NOVEMBER 1864

NEW STYLE HEAD-DRESS.

PETERSON'S MAGAZINE
DECEMBER 1864

GENERAL REMARKS.—HEAD-DRESSES are mostly in the *Watteau* style. The horns *a la Russe*, which have made so many of our belles look like those huge horned caterpillars, are no longer worn. The hair is crimped and banded loosely back from the forehead, or worn in small ringlets.

Flowers are arranged in small bunches and tufts for the hair, and placed on the head in the style the most becoming to the wearer.

GODEY'S LADY'S BOOK
JANUARY 1865

CHITCHAT UPON NEW YORK AND PHILADELPHIA FASHIONS FOR JANUARY.

Birds of all sizes are used in great profusion on most everything, and frequently the effect is both stylish and good. We find at the Maison Tilman, 148 East Ninth Street, New York, some charming coiffures for young ladies. They consist of two tufts of flowers, one for the back and one for the front of the head joined by ribbons. A very graceful one was of silver wheat-ears mounted with thick stems of blue velvet tipped with silver. The two bunches were connected by blue velvet which fell in loops and ends at the back. Gold wheat was mounted with green velvet in the same way. Another very stylish head dress was of scarlet velvet with a cluster of thistles at the side, and a trailing branch of dark glossy leaves fell at the back.

Colossal roses are now very much worn on bonnets; these, though unnatural in size, are exquisitely beautiful. Dewdrops are very plentiful, so also are icicles, and hoar frost is seen covering many of the leaves. The latter is very popular for evening coiffures, as It has a charming effect by gas-light. Bugs of various descriptions find their way to the hearts or leaves of most all the roses.

The greatest perfection is now attained in artificial flowers, and all have the bright, soft, or lustrous shades peculiar to the originals.

Particular attention is now paid to the green leaves. We see them changing with all the lively autumnal tints, or else soft and velvety. Imperfect and dying leaves are also very much admired, and are successfully employed for all the choicest garnitures.

The ball coiffures at this establishment are very lovely. Most of them consist of a large tuft with a garland falling loosely at the back, while soft thick stems are twined round, the head, keeping the wreath in form. Thick stems of velvet are very much used; pink flowers are mounted on green velvet, and white flowers on blue or scarlet.

Butterflies continue to be a popular ornament, and are made of jet, gilt gauze, colored mother of pearl, and gauze lined with tinsel, while the more costly are studded with jewels.

Novelties are constantly appearing in the show-rooms of the Maison Tilman, and a very charming one is a head-dress of velvet in the shape of a shell, from which are escaping marine plants and grasses. The shell is studded and looped with pearls which fall on the neck.

THE LADY'S FRIEND
JANUARY 1865

GENERAL REMARKS.—LACE HEAD-DRESSES are also fashionable ; the lappets commence at the top of the head, cross, and the two ends fall upon the neck. A flower is placed upon the neck, and another at the side, upon the bandeau of hair. This is the style of almost all the head-dresses this season ; the high fantastic ornaments being quite abandoned. The newest flowers are not copied from nature ; they are very original, and when made with taste are highly effective. The large shells, made of shaded velvet with marine plants, grasses, and pearls escaping from them, are among the most popular head-dresses of the season.

For the sprays of flowers on flexible stems which are occasionally worn as coronets on the front of the head, the smallest kinds are used, such as violets, daisies and hawthorn.

PETERSON'S MAGAZINE
JANUARY 1865

GENERAL REMARKS.—HEAD-DRESSES, for young ladies, consist of nets scattered over with gold, steel, coral, or jet beads. Flowers are placed on the hair in detached bunches, sometimes only a sing rose being employed. Wreaths are no longer seen.

PETERSON'S MAGAZINE
FEBRUARY 1865

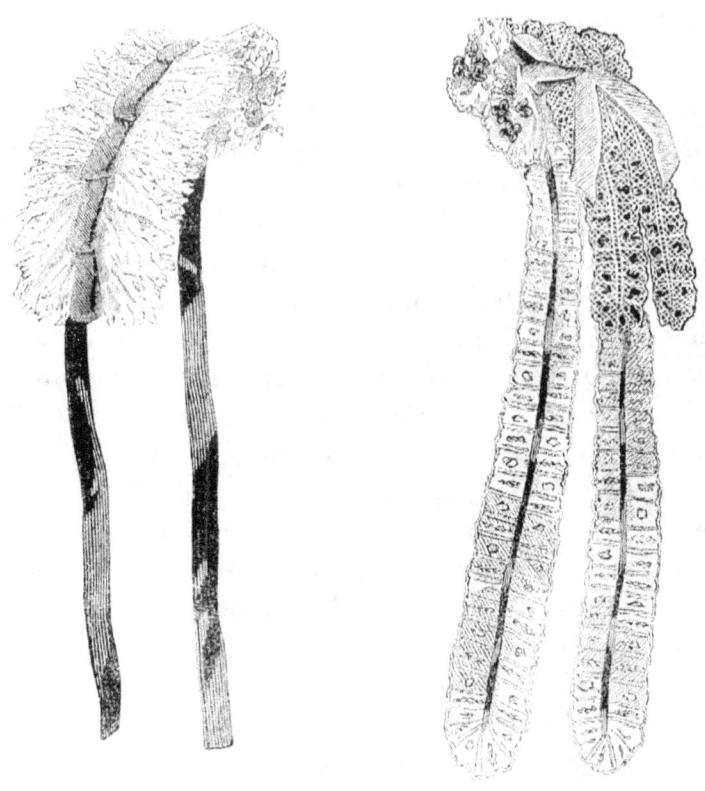

HEAD-DRESSES.

Fig. 8.

Fig. 10.

Fig. 10 is an evening coiffure. Round the head a very narrow quilling of velvet ; at the right side, bows of black velvet and *glacé* ribbon *couleur de rose ;* in the front a large moss-rose, buds, and foliage.

Fig 8.—Fancy coiffure, formed of blonde lace, with loops of pink velvet down the centre. Over the forehead are full bunches of pink flowers. The streamers are of black velvet.

CHITCHAT UPON NEW YORK AND PHILADELPHIA FASHIONS FOR MARCH.

We think that the devotees of Fashion cannot help being pleased with the charming collection of Parisian novelties at the Maison Tilman of 148 East Ninth Street, New York. Among the numerous elegant coiffures, we were attracted by one formed of a branch of tempting-looking straw-berries, with rich green foliage mounted on gilt stems. At the back was a shower of golden grasses, intended to veil the chignon or waterfall. For young ladies there are many graceful little coiffures, such, for instance, as the Eugenie. This is formed of a tuft of roses and forget-me-nots for the centre of the head, another for the back, from which falls a garland of rosebuds seemingly dripping with dew. Most of the coiffures are composed of separate tufts or branches, or else of flexible garlands, which can be twined in with puffs and curls to great advantage. Other styles for young ladies are of blonde flowers mounted on ordinary stems, a very graceful style, and particularly adapted to the light evening dresses now so very popular. Others, again, are of white flowers without foliage, and many of flowers and ribbons intermingled. The mixture of tulle with flowers proves so very becoming, that it is adopted by both young and elderly ladies. Large bows of tulle are also worn at the throat.

CHITCHAT UPON NEW YORK AND PHILADELPHIA FASHIONS FOR APRIL.

As headdresses are in requisition during the entire year, we cannot do better than give a description of some very novel and elegant ones just received at the Mason Tilman, 148 East Math Street, New York.

The "Joan of Arc" is composed of superb crimson carnations festooned with small chains, and ornamented with long strings of small steel beads.

The "Empress" is made with a fall front spray of white Persian lilacs, surrounded by blue forget-me-nots. On this spray is a blue enameled dragon-fly, and the long branch of white lilacs drooping over the shoulder, is dotted over with blue enameled insects.

The "Regent" consists of the most beautiful passion flowers, surrounded by the softest green feather gross sparkling with large diamond ornaments. One is placed in the centre of the flower over the forehead, the others are suspended by delicate crystal chains.

The "Princesse" is made of Mexican blue velvet an inch wide, arranged in clusters of loops, with long ends. A wide bow composed of threads of spun gold is arranged with brilliant effect to take the place of a comb at the back. A circlet of gold braided and fastened with slender pendent ornaments, gives a very novel and distingue appearance to the front.

Headdresses are also ornamented with jet and pearl ornaments shaped like daggers, crescents, or tassels. Diamond and crescent shaped nets with a pendent fringe, are now used for the front of headdresses, the fringe falling over the forehead.

PETERSON'S MAGAZINE
APRIL 1865

HEAD-DRESS.

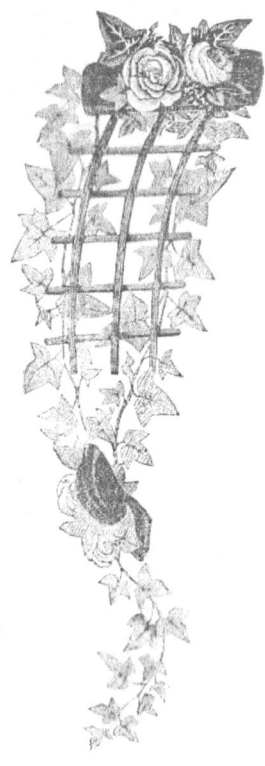

HEAD-DRESS of ivy and roses ; the trellis of black velvet.

GENERAL REMARKS.—The simple velvet bands, with a bow at the side of the head—a popular style—are made of piece velvet, cut on the cross ; an eighth of a yard will be found a sufficient quantity for the purpose. A band should first be made, which, when finished, should measure one inch in width ; this should be lined with stiff net, and fastened round the head with a button. A bow, with two ends, resembling a tie, should be added at the left side ; the bow must be studded over with beads. If scarlet velvet is used, black beads will look the best ; if black velvet, the white satin beads form a good contrast ; and if blue velvet is found becoming to the complexion, then either gilt or silver beads may be employed. The beads should be dotted over the bow when it is formed, and should not be studded too thickly together. This is the simplest style of head-dress for home wear. A more dressy style are the velvet covers for the back hair. These are made either of turquoise blue, or bright scarlet velvet studded with gold beads. They are fastened to a tortoiseshell comb with an ornamental gilt top, and are so made that they encase the entire puff of hair at the back. An elastic is introduced in such a way as to draw them into the form of a small net. Those who have no great quantity of hair, will find these velvet covers very advantageous. They are rendered more elegant by adding two gold tassels behind the left ear.

The small Louis XV. wreaths or circlets of flowers are popular among young ladies, who wear them at the summit of the tiers of bandeaux which now crown their heads when in full dress.

Fig. 8.

CHITCHAT UPON NEW YORK AND PHILADEL-PHIA FASHIONS FOR MAY.

In lieu of the net, some married ladies have adopted a bag of bright silk or velvet, either plain or ornamented with beads. These are drawn into the form of a net by an elastic, and fastened to a comb, taking the place of the waterfall. It Is a convenient and dressy style of coiffure, and as the bag can be stuffed with a roll or horse-hair, it is of but little consequence if Nature has been sparing of her gifts.

Fig. 8.—Coiffure of rose-colored velvet, with a wide barbe of black lace.

THE LADY'S FRIEND
MAY 1865

GENERAL REMARKS.—A style of head-dress has lately been introduced which it would not be difficult for amateurs to manufacture at home. A piece of velvet four yards in length, and an inch and a half in breadth, is procured. This is studded over at regular distances with small pink rose-buds. A bow is then formed and placed in the centre of the forehead, among the bandeaux ; the ribbon is carried round the sides of the head, and tied as though it fastened the plaits and the back, and the ends float to the waist ; a filigree gold butterfly is placed in the centre of the bow in front.

It is not elaborate, but it has a very pleasing effect with a white tulle or tarlatane dress.

A very fashionable style of coiffure is a bandeaux of colored velvet, over which are fastened ornaments of gold, steel, or crystal, or sprigs of artificial flowers. They do not look much when laid on the table, but are extremely pretty and effective when skillfully arranged and twisted within bows and plaits of hair, brown or golden.

Fig. 11.

Fig. 12.

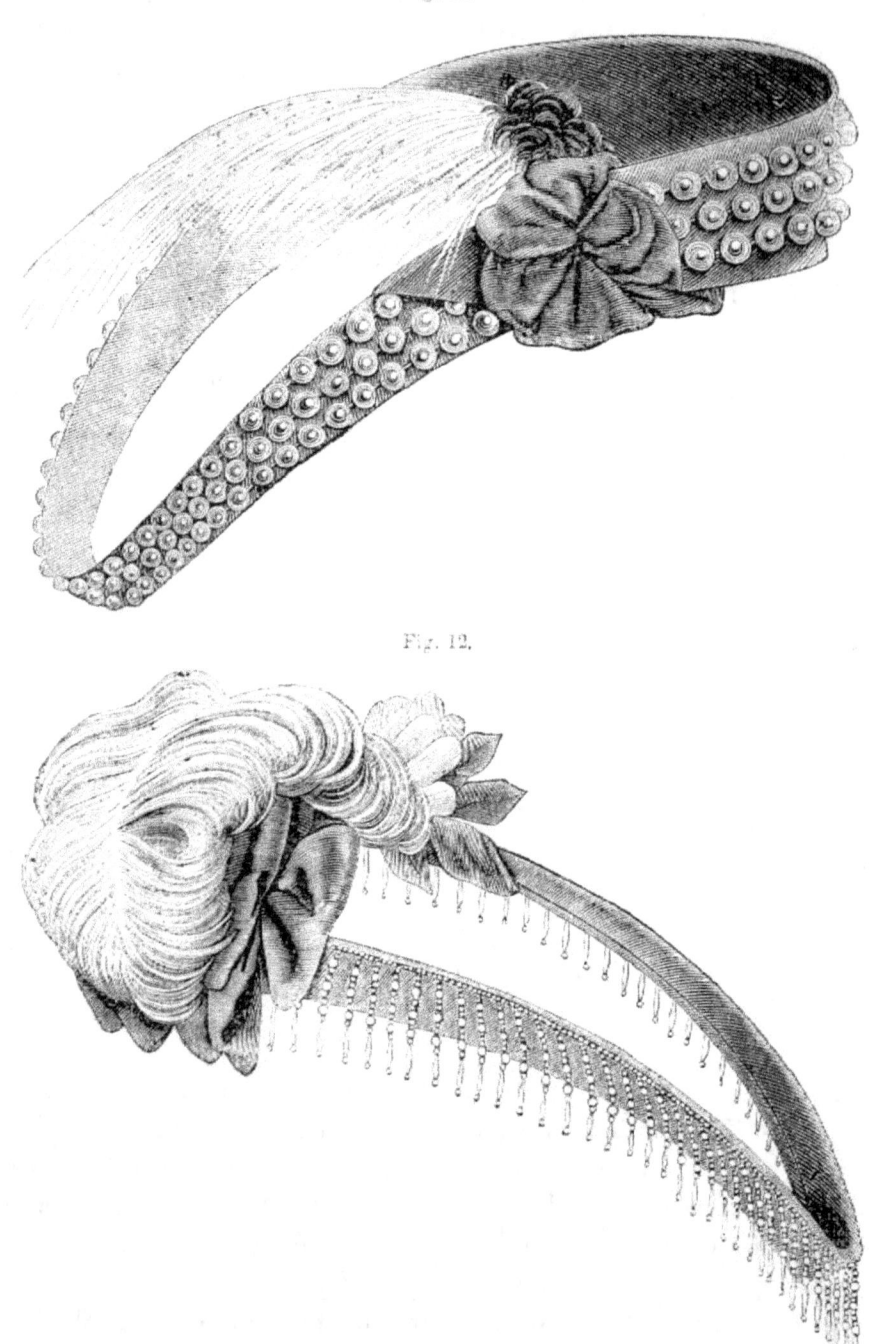

Fig. 11.—Coiffure Diadème. This is a rich blue velvet, studded with pearl beads of different sizes. On one side is a rosette of blue velvet, a short blue feather, and a long white plume.

Fig. 12.—Coiffure Astrèe. The coiffure is formed of rose-colored velvet, covered with a fringe of pearl beads. In front is a long white plume, loops of rose-colored velvet, and leaves of mother-of pearl.

GODEY'S LADY'S BOOK
AUGUST 1865

CHITCHAT UPON NEW YORK AND PHILADEL-PHIA FASHIONS FOR AUGUST.

The noticeable feature of floral coiffures is that they are all of the *bandalette* style. We noticed, however, a very-charming little Nea-politan headdress made of lace and pointed on the forehead. The lappet at the back was divided into two narrow ends, the whole ornamented with small flies of gold and enamel on bows of scarlet velvet.

THE LADY'S FRIEND
AUGUST 1865

The generality of head-dresses are made with bandelets ; wreaths are only to be seen occasionally. A very fashionable headdress is called the *Norma* ; the hair is turned back from the temples *à l'antique*, and is crowned with a double bandelet of foliage (oak, willow, laurel, or ivy : generally willow leaves are selected). This foliage is mounted on gold branches, and these gold stems form a large network at the back of the head.

GODEY'S LADY'S BOOK
SEPTEMBER 1865

CHITCHAT UPON NEW YORK AND PHILADEL-PHIA FASHIONS FOR SEPTEMBER.

The newest headdresses are formed of plates of silver, steel, or enamel, arranged as a band passing round the head and forming a *cache peine*, or long, flat cross-piece for the back of the head, finished with chains and beads. A very graceful headdress is formed of a thick, rope-like gilt cord, knotted at intervals round the head and falling at the side with two rich gilt tassels.

THE LADY'S FRIEND
OCTOBER 1865

EVENING HEAD-DRESS.—This head-dress is composed of two pieces of lace, laid on each other, and covered with a velvet ribbon, terminated in front with a double bow, and behind with a tuft of loops. A large rose with foliage is placed in the middle, and completes the coiffure.

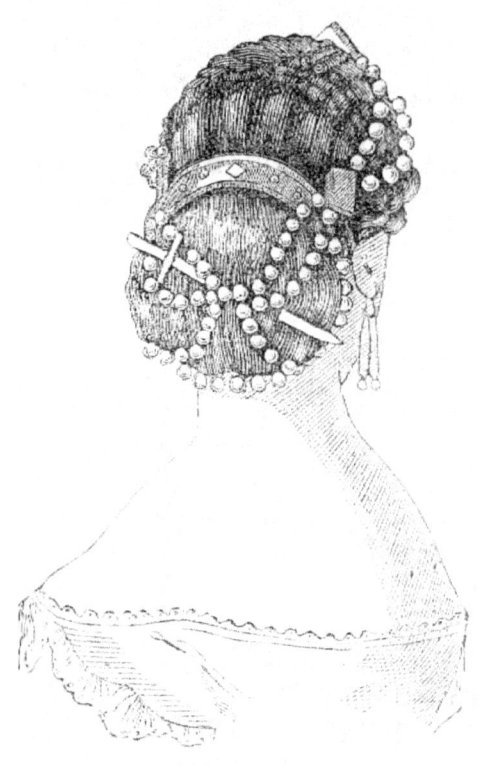

BALL HEAD-DRESS.

HEAD-DRESS.

GODEY'S LADY'S BOOK
NOVEMBER 1865

CHITCHAT UPON NEW YORK AND PHILADELPHIA FASHIONS FOR NOVEMBER.

Headdresses are all in the Greek style, either fillets of velvet studded with beads, or stars of gilt, silver, or steel, or else they are hung with chains of gilt sequins. For full dress, these bandelettes or fillets are composed of delicate flowers mounted on gilt stems, with green leaves edged and veined with gold. The artistic blending of gold with the beautiful flowers and foliage renders the colors perfectly charming.

A NEAPOLITAN HEAD-DRESS.—It is a square made of Maltese insertion, edged with Maltese lace. A row of groseille ribbon is placed over the joining of the insertion and lace. A *pouf* of groseille velvet in the front.

GENERAL REMARKS.—Bandelets in the hair, with steel stars on them, are all the rage at present ; they are not embroidered on the velvet, but are made separately, and sewn down upon it ; they sparkle at candlelight, and are wonderfully effective in the hair. The bandelets can now be purchased either ready-mounted or as ribbon. The ribbon is preferable, because it can be added easily to any arrangement of hair. When the hair is dressed, the ribbon can be bound three times round the head, whether the *bandeaux* be flat or puffed out, *crépés* or plain—with all styles the three bandelets are worn. They are as frequently studded with gold and silver as with steel stars. Silver produces a soft and pleasing effect on sky-blue velvet. Straw stars are frequently to be seen also on these bandelets.

EMPIRE HEAD-DRESSES.

THESE Greek Head-Dresses, or "Bandelets," as they are called in these modern times, are made in every variety of material. Those for very full dress are made of solid bands of treble gilt, either burnished or frosted ; sometimes the front band is ornamented with little gilt sequins to match, bands of cut steel are, also, very brilliant ; they usually have hairpins to correspond, which seem to be used to fasten the "Bandelets" with. In our engraving we give the "Bandelet" made of velvet, ornamented with beads. To make one, eighth of a yard of velvet, but bias, is required ; divide this into three equal parts, cutting the velvet on the bias, of course. Sew the edges of the velvet together with a slip-stitch, so that the stitches may not show upon the right side ; make the three bands, graduating them to fit the head. Ornament with wax beads in imitation of pearls ; or with gilt or steel beads. A narrow taffetas ribbon, sewed at each end

of the "Bandelet," is the most convenient way of fastening the head-dress, as it then can be more easily adjusted in its proper place. Of course, it is understood that the hair is to be entirely denuded of the puffs and frizettes so long worn, and is to be dressed quite close to the head.

GENERAL REMARKS.—HEAD-DRESSES have also changed completely since last spring. The huge waterfall, which used to hang down the back, soiling the dresses, and making short-necked people look as if the head was set directly on the shoulders, has been discarded, and is now made smaller in rounder form, and is placed quite high at the back of thead. In some cases it is worn much higher than represented in our engravings, though they show the usual style. This "*chignon*," as it is termed, is no longer combed smoothly, as it used to be, over frizettes, but is crimped, or composed of plaits, or *short*

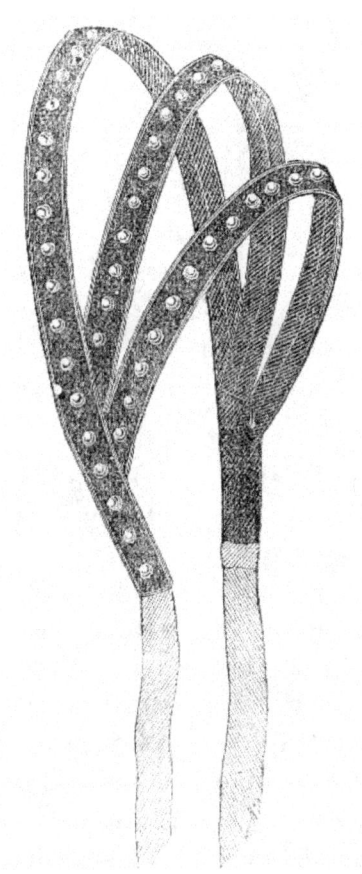

ringlets. The front hair is sometimes arranged with small tufts of curls on the top of the fore-head, and sometimes with a row of tiny curls all around the face, which may, or may not pass around the back of the head under the *chignon.* Sometimes the hair is combed entire-ly back, and only ornamented with a braid passed like a coronet, around the front. But for evening dress the curls are more popular.

BANDELETS, OR FILLETS, as they are some-times called, are made of ribbon, or velvet, studded with gold, jet, or pearl beads, accord-ing to the dress with which they are worn. Some of the more expensive ones are made of gilt, silver, or steal bands. For a party-dress, one flower is placed at the side of the head.

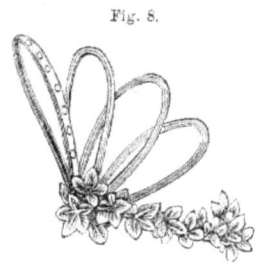

Fig. 8—Evening headdress, composed of circlets of Ponceau velvet ; the front one covered
by a gold band, and the one at the back covered by a garland of ivy leaves with gold veins.

CHITCHAT UPON NEW YORK AND PHILADELPHIA FASHIONS FOR DECEMBER.

The most fashionable headdresses—except for full dress—consist of three narrow bands of velvet ornamented with spangles, beads, or small drops of pearl, gilt, steel, or crystal. These bands are tied with a ribbon just under the waterfall. Gilt bands of different sizes and styles also come for the same purpose; they can be bought ready made or by the strip. Some have a fringe of fancy drops, others arc studded with pearl or coral.

Gilt sequins are arranged as fringes and worn on head-dresses, veils, and bonnets; they also depend from the centre of silk buttons, and are exceedingly stylish. The fashionable veil is termed the Sultan, and Is one yard long and about three-quarters wide. It is of plain or figured net, simply hemmed and headed by gilt or pearl gimp, or else trimmed with a lace or inserting. It is thrown on the side of the bonnet when not over the face, and is really very stylish.

THE LADY'S FRIEND
DECEMBER 1865

EMPIRE COIFFURE.—This coiffure is composed of three rolls of ribbon, supported by steel springs. The first roll forms a bandeau over the forehead, and is hidden at the sides by the hair, which is much waved and combed up. The two ends are fastened behind and flow on the shoulders. The two other rolls are put on the top of the head, and joined together by an elastic.

GENERAL REMARKS.—Bandalets continue to be in high favor. Young ladies wear colored velvet-ribbon for the daytime : this is placed between the *bandeaux*, crosses the top of the head, the two ends are then joined to form a careless bow on the *chignon*, and precisely at the top of the comb. It is a simple, graceful style, and convenient under a hat.

NETS

GODEY'S LADY'S BOOK
JANUARY 1860

A BORDERED NET FOR SLEEPING IN.

BORDERED NET FOR SLEEPING IN.

Materials.—Nos. 16 and 20 cotton ; two meshes—one flat that will measure in width three-eighths of and inch, and a round mesh that will measure the same in a piece of string put round it.

LARGEST mesh, 16 cotton ; net on a foundation of 16 stitches, 32 rows or 16 diamonds counted perpendicularly ; cut the foundation away, do not cut off the end of cotton ; tie a piece of string in the centre of this square of netting ; now net all round the square, being careful not to net two stiches into any corner loop ; net twelve rounds of 6 diamonds ; do not fasten off.

FOR THE BORDER.—With 20 cotton and large mesh, net three loops in every stitch.

Small mesh, 3 rows.

Small mesh, 6 stitches in each alternate loop

Small mesh, 2 rows.

Small mesh, net 5 stitches, miss the connecting loop between the two groups of stitches, net 5, miss the loop again ; repeats.

Next row.—Net 4 stitches, miss the loop over the same loop as in last row, and repeat.

Next row.—Net 3 miss the loop as before.

Last row.— Net 2, miss the loop as before ; there will now be one diamond over each group of stitches.

BEAD AND CROCHET HAIR NET.
BY MRS. JANE WEAVER.

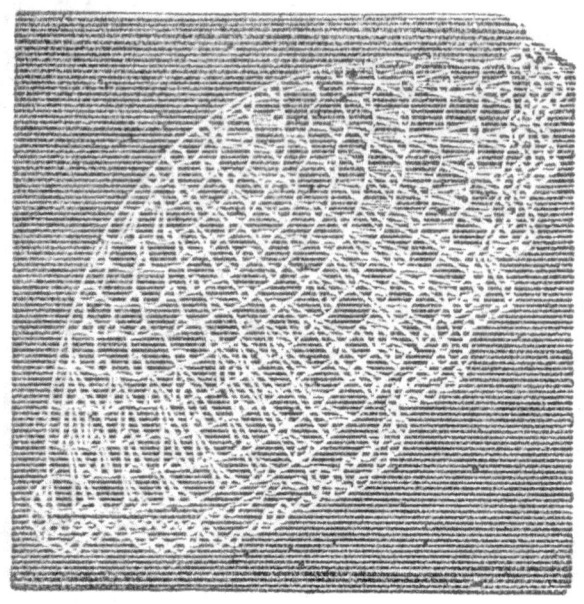

MATERIALS.—6 skeins sadler or purse silk. Black, 3 oz. Jet beads. Fine steel hook.

Thread the beads upon the silk, then make a ch of 6. Join and into it work 6 dc stitches, with 4 ch between each stitch, putting in a bead at every stitch. This for the 1st row. Then work 7 rows in dc (treble crochet) stitch, with 4 ch between each stitch, widening enough to keep the work flat, one bead at every stitch as before. 8th row, * 1 dc, 1 bead 2 ch, 1 bead 2 ch, 4 dc together, (1 bead between 2nd and 3rd stitches,0 2 ch, 1 bead, 2 ch, * all round. 9th, 10th, 11th rows same as 8th row, only observing 3 ch, 1 bead, 3 ch between the stitches instead of 2 ch, 1 bead, 2 ch, as in the 8th row.

For the 1st row of border, thread 30 beads, loop as close as the fancy may suggest. 2nd row, 40 beads, looped directly under the loops of 1st row. The number of beads for these loops depends upon the size, or course. The loops, however, should be 3 inches in length for the 1st row: 4 inches for the 2nd. An elastic cord or braid ran in the last row of work, completes the net.

Let it be remembered, in crocheting, that the manner of working, by different persons, varies materially, some persons drawing the stitches through very lightly, others quite the opposite. In following a pattern, some little allowance can be made by the person working, such as adding another ch stitch in any place, if the work should draw, or narrowing 1 stitch should it be too full. In the above design, it is requisite to keep the work flat. After the 7th row, the widening must all be done in the ch stitches, adding one or more, as the work may seem to need it. To a person who crochets tightly, it may be necessary to add a row or more to the work to make the net large enough.

NETTED NET FOR THE HAIR
BY MRS. JANE WEAVER

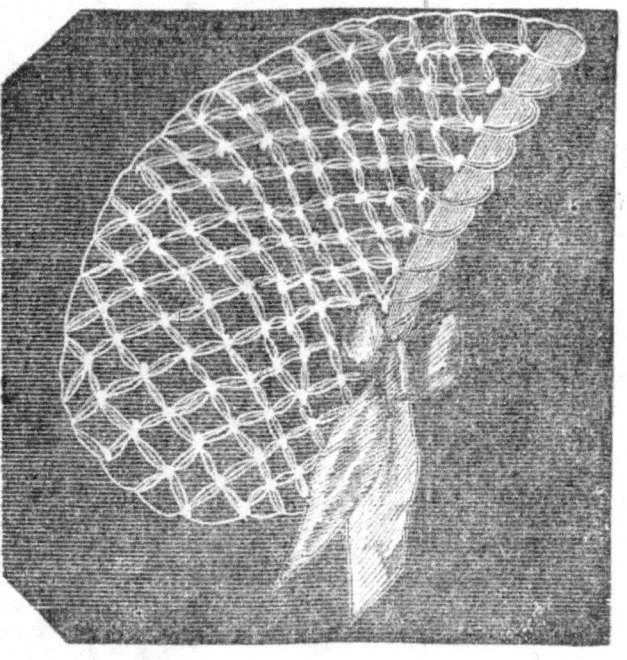

MATERIALS.--One dozen pieces narrow silk floss braid, 1–¼ yards of ribbon, mesh ½ inch wide, mesh one inch wide, large bone netting needle.

1st Row.—Use the small mesh, and work 9 stitches in plain diamond netting.

2nd Row.—Widen 1 stitch at each end of row.

3rd and 4th rows same as 2nd row.

Net 12 rows without widening.

Net 3 rows, narrowing 1 stitch at the beginning and end of each row. 1 row plain. Use the large mesh, and net 1 row all around the work, into this row run the ribbon. Tie with bow and ends at the side.

This is the latest novelty in nets for the hair. They are very becoming when made of dark-blue, brown, or black braid, with ribbon to match, prettily tied at the side. We have designed it expressly for the readers of "Peterson."

FANCY HEADDRESS.

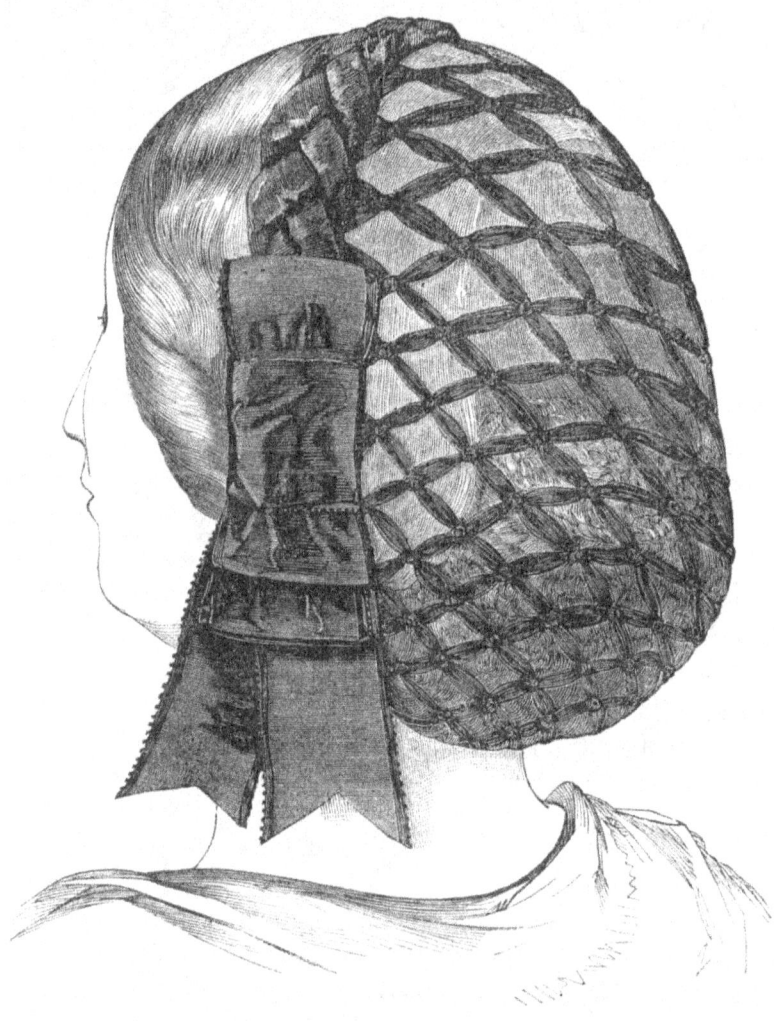

This net is made of chenille, silk, or braid. A plait of velvet is placed round it, and at the side a velvet bow.

A CHENILLE NET FOR THE HAIR.

Materials.—One skein of colored or brown silk chenille, such as is sold for making hair nets ; a flat mesh, one inch in width ; and a small wooden, or large steel, netting-needle.

Net six loops on a foundation ; then net twelve rows ; these will count six diamonds.

Cut the netting from the foundation, but not cut off the chenille. Tie a loop of cotton into the centre of the square of chenille ; then net round the square six rows, or three diamonds, or more, if required.

PETERSON'S MAGAZINE
APRIL 1860

NET FOR HAIR.

GODEY'S LADY'S BOOK
SEPTEMBER 1860

Fig. 4 is a net for the hair, of double silk, with a braid of velvet ribbon around and large flat loops and ends to the right ; a gold cord is looped with he velvet ribbon, and gold fringe finishes the ornament.

PETERSON'S MAGAZINE
DECEMBER 1860

GENERAL REMARKS.—NETS are still worn both in neglige and full dress. Some have every mesh covered by a little gold star; others are entirely of gold with a small coronet of *pompons* forming a bandeau; and other again are made of large cords of silk. A beautiful net made lately to wear with white dress trimmed with daisies, had the meshes composed of very small daisies.

GODEY'S LADY'S BOOK
JANUARY 1861

Figs. 7 and 8.—Black velvet net for the hair, with four heavy tassels in gold.

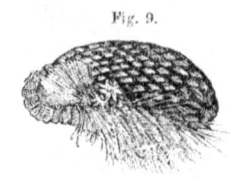

Fig. 9.—Chenille net for the hair, with a bunch of aquatic grasses, an thin blossoms in gold.

PETERSON'S MAGAZINE
MARCH 1861

GENERAL REMARKS.—NETS still continue to be worn trimmed with ruched ribbon, bows, or tassels, and are made in gold, lace, and chenille, although the latter have become almost too general to considered very *recherché.* For the theatre or a dinner party, a pretty little head-dress may be made of a bandeau of cerise or Magenta velvet about the thickness of the little finger. Rosettes of white blonde, and roses without leaves, placed alternately, should form the coronet, and the rosettes and roses should increase in size and number toward the back of the head-dress.

GODEY'S LADY'S BOOK
MAY 1861

CHITCHAT UPON NEW YORK AND PHILADELPHIA FASHIONS FOR MAY.
Nets for the hair are by no means laid aside ; they are still very much worn in morning-dress, and also in evening *negligé.* Those made of colored chenille or velvet are very becoming ; they are usually finished with tassels or rosettes.

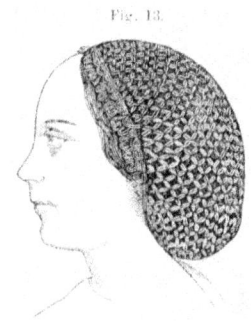

Fig.13.—Net made of thick chenille.

CHITCHAT UPON NEW YORK AND PHILADEL-PHIA FASHIONS FOR AUGUST.

NETS for the HAIR are as much adopted as ever. The prettiest are made of chenille, with a trimming in the form of a coronet. The "Clotilde" is the newest style of net yet introduced. It is formed of black or brown chenille, with a large bow of ribbon above the forehead. This description of net is worn by the Princess Clotilde for in-door neglige dress, and thence it has received its name.

GODEY'S LADY'S BOOK
DECEMBER 1861

INVISIBLE HAIRNETS.

As there are still many ladies who value the comfort and convenience of the hair-net, and who are desirous of retaining it as long as fashion permits, we are very happy to comply with the wish of a subscriber, and give instructions for making the newest that has appeared, which is one that bears the name of the "Invisible Hair-Net." As its title implies, this net is scarcely distinguishable when worn upon the hair, as it matches it in color, and is also remarkably fine and clear, the meshes being open. The silk used is much finer than the finest netting silk, and is strong, being a sort of raw silk. Commence by making twenty loops on a mesh one-third of an inch wide, and net as many rows, thus forming a perfect square, then gather up a little portion of the centre of this square, tie it round and attach it to the string of the netting stirrup, and then continue to net all round the edge of the square until the desired size has been reached. This size must be regulated according to the convenience of the proposed wearer, and this must depend upon the quantity of hair which it is intended to confine. When completed, an elastic must be passed through the last row of loops ; the net must be moistened with a little weak gum-water, stretched over a dinner-plate, and left to dry. These invisible hair-nets are the best that have been introduced, and are, in fact, the only kind now worn.

PETERSON'S MAGAZINE
DECEMBER 1861

NET FOR THE HAIR

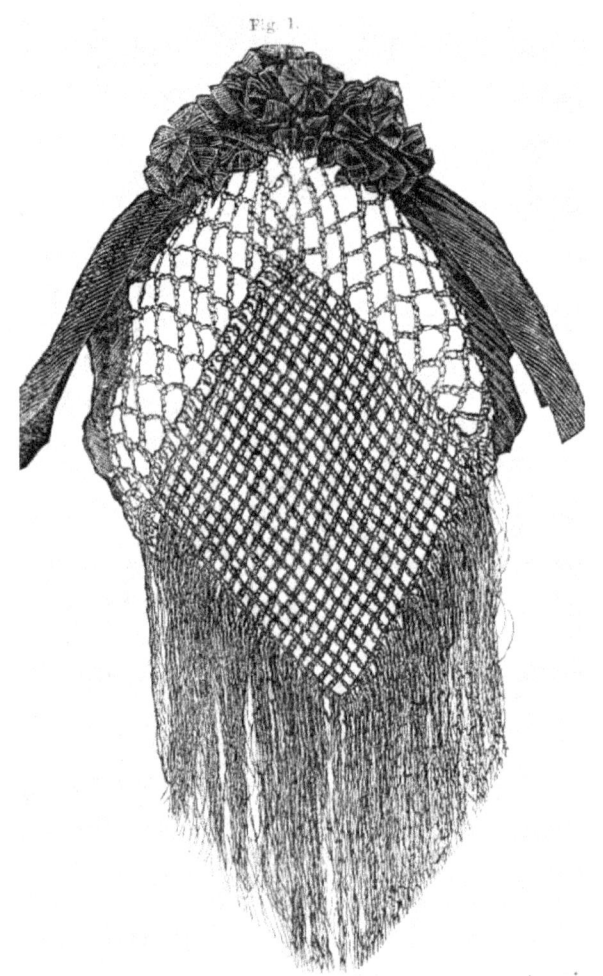

Fig. 1.

HEADDRESS.

Fig. 1.—*Crochet Headdress.*—This pretty little coiffure is suitable for morning wear, and is extremely easy to make. It is composed of purse silk, and trimmed with a coronet of bows and ends of black velvet The back is made in the following manner: -

Make a chain of 60 stitches, and work a square of treble crochet, putting 2 chain between each treble. Then, for the top of the headdress, crochet on two sides of the square, 7 chain, and loop into every other treble. Repeat this for five rows, and mount this portion of the net on a pointed wire. Ornament it with bows and ends of velvet tastefully arranged, and finish off the back by lengths of silk looped in to form a fringe. About eight lengths of silk are required for one loop of fringe .

This might be converted into an evening headdress by making the foundation in some bright colored silk, or gold twist, and ornamenting the front with small white ostrich feathers .

Fig. 5.

FIG. VI.—BLACK NET. Trimmed with loops and rosettes made of very narrow pink ribbon.

GODEY'S LADY'S BOOK
OCTOBER 1862

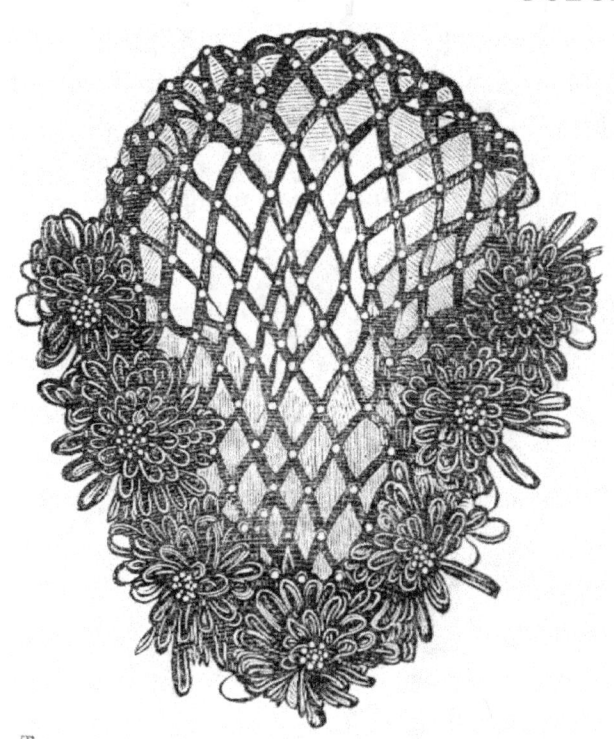

BLACK VELVET NET,
ORNAMENTED WITH ROSETTES AND PEARL BEADS.

The materials required for one net are ; two pieces of very narrow black velvet, two rows of small sized imitation pearl beads, seven pearl stars (or ornamental buttons might be used). Seven rosettes with pearl centres ornament the front, which should be mounted on a piece of pointed wire, the net being fastened to this wire. A small piece of elastic should be run in behind, fastened on each side to the end of the wire Should our readers not care about purchasing the ready made stars by exercising a little ingenuity they may easily arrange a few beads in the form of a star for the centre of the rosettes .

GODEY'S LADY'S BOOK
NOVEMBER 1862

Fig. 4.

Fig. 4.—Headdress, formed of a gold net and scarlet and gold rosettes, with scarlet velvet bow and ends.

GODEY'S LADY'S BOOK
MARCH 1863

Fig. 2.

Fig. 2.—Coiffure composed of a gold net and a roll of lobelia blue velvet, twined with a gold cord and tassel.

GODEY'S LADY'S BOOK
APRIL 1863

Fig. 4.—Rich coiffure, made of a gold net, with a torsade of black velvet, and trimmed with bunches of gold leaves.

GODEY'S LADY'S BOOK
SEPTEMBER 1863

CHITCHAT UPON NEW YORK AND PHILADEL-
PHIA FASHIONS FOR SEPTEMBER.

A new style of net has been introduced. It made of hair the exact shade of the wearer's. It is netted over a fine mesh, which makes it almost invisible and very durable.

PETERSON'S MAGAZINE
NOVEMBER 1863

GENERAL REMARKS.—For MORNING WEAR, the nets which are so generally worn are all trimmed with a bow at the top of the head. This is an improvement upon the elastic which, when visible, was not a pretty object to contemplate; the unformal bow now completely conceals the elastic. The loops should run along the top, and the ribbon should be of the same color as the net, and not wide.

PETERSON'S MAGAZINE
DECEMBER 1863

GODEY'S LADY'S BOOK
DECEMBER 1863
CHITCHAT UPON NEW YORK AND PHILADELPHIA FASHIONS FOR DECEMBER.

Among the novelties in leather we find leather nets. They are formed of narrow strips caught together in diamonds by steel, jet, or gilt beads, and trimmed with ruches and ribbons. Sometimes the leather is of the natural hue, at other times it is colored. Another pretty style has bright silk cords twined in with the leather, which in quite an improvement. Then we have fancy leather cuffs, finished with silk and leather ruching, suitable and pretty for travelling or street wear.

The little bows composed of silk and leather are also very stylish, and are in great variety of shape and color. They are generally mounted on pins, so as to make them exceedingly convenient. Another novelty is the *aumoniére*, a fancy leather pouch or bag, worn at the side, and merely large enough to contain a purse or handkerchief. It resembles the bag on page 298 of the March number.

GENERAL REMARKS.—THERE IS A NEW STYLE OF HAIR-NETS; they are made of thick twisted cord with velvet or chenille flowers in the front, and from each side two ribbons are carried round to the back where they are tied in a large bow which falls on to the neck. For this style the hair must not be arranged too low at the back. Ribbons have never been manufactured with so much taste as is at present displayed in them, and no dress is sent hom unaccompanied by an immensely wide sash.

HAIR NETS

Nets for the hair being much worn at the present season, we have chosen a few of the most fashionable for illustration, and as several of our subscribers have written for patterns of this description, we have given directions for both useful and ornamental nets.

The Marie Louise is an entirely new design, the ornamental part being formed of narrow bands of Russia leather, secured with steel beads ; the front is trimmed with small stars, worked in tatting, and of the same color as the bands. The net is of Alexander Blue Braid, or, if preferred, black may be substituted ; and it can of course be made in any color, but blue or black harmonizes best with the ornaments.

MATERIALS.—For the net, a piece of colored braid, a large netting needle, and a flat mesh three-quarters of an inch in width. For the trimming, a

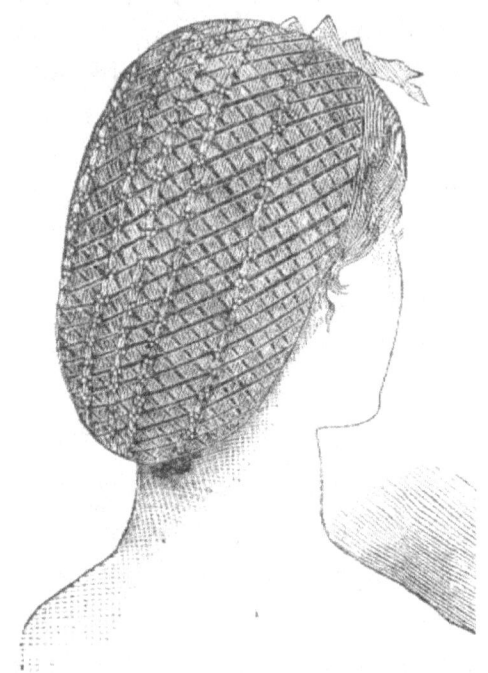

bunch of steel beads, No. 9, and seven bands of narrow Russia leather, which are usually sold twelve inches in length, and are stamped with a small gimp pattern. For the stars, a skein of tatting twine the color of pin. To trim the front, one and a half yards wide, and one yard one inch wide. Also one yard of elastic.

THE NET.

Commence on a foundation of 8 stitches (this will make a large size), work backwards and forwards for 16 rows in plain netting ; take it off the foundation, and stretch it open, when it will form a square, which is for the centre of the net ; the following rounds being worked on the edges of this square, to do which a foundation thread should be run along the four sides a few stitches from the edge ; then work down the selvedge formed by the side of the rows, netting a stitch in each of the seven loops ; at the corner, increase by netting 2 stitches in one stitch ; then net along the first row, and repeat all round, increasing at each corner.

Net 10 rounds plain, and fasten off. The

elastic is to be run in the last round.

To ornament the net see small figure. Take a band, and, commencing on one of the knots formed by the stitches of the net, sew the band to it, then thread on six beads and pass them across in a slanting direction, taking a stitch in the net to secure it ; then thread 6 more beads, and placing them across the first 6, secure them, and fasten off.

Work the same at each knot straight across the netting to the opposite side. Attach two more bands parallel with the first and on each diamond of the netting ; then a fourth band, leaving two diamonds of the net between, and a fifth band on the other side of the first, leaving two diamonds between to correspond with the other side.

THE STARS (in Tatting).—Fill the shuttle with the twine, and, commencing a loop, work a double stitch, then (1 pearl loop and 2 double stitches alternately, 7 times) ; 1 pearl and 1 double more, draw the loop quite close, place the two ends together, knot them, and cut off the twine. Make 22 of these stars.

Take about eight inches of wide ribbon wire, and cover it with the narrow blue ribbon, placing the wire in the centre of it, so as to leave equal lengths at each end for strings ; these are tied at the back of the net, and the part with the wire sewed to about ten stitches of the net.

Take the wide ribbon, double it so as to commence in the middle, and at one edge make a plait or fold so as to form the point in the centre ; make two loops or bows on each side of the centre, and leaving a longer space between them, make two more bows ; the rest of the ribbon is for the ends. The stars should now be tucked on, placing three beads in the centre of each ; this ribbon is then attached to the band in the front.

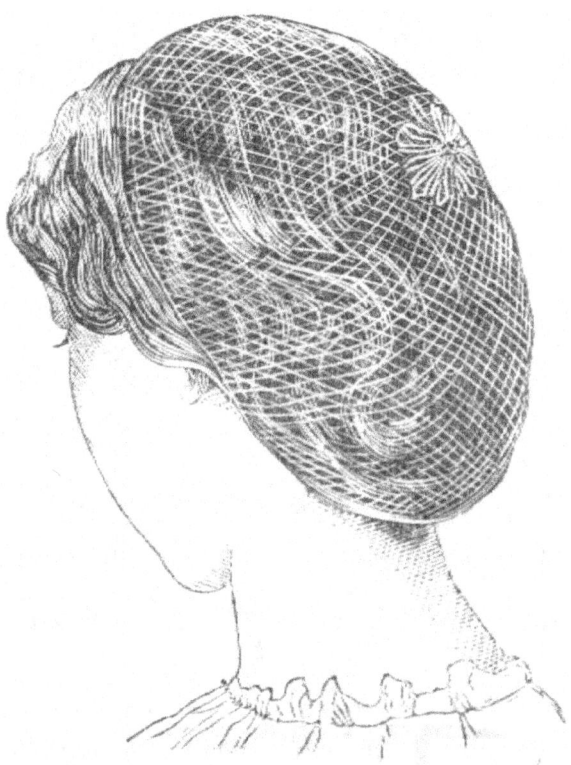

SIMPLE SLEEPING NET.

Materials.—Crochet cotton, No. 2 ; a flat mesh a quarter of an inch in width, and a netting needle. Narrow cotton braid may also be used.

Commence on a foundation of 50 stitches, net them, and make it round by working a stitch in the first stitch ; then net 25 rounds quite plain.

27th round.—Decrease, by netting every two stitches together as one stitch.

28th.—All plain.

29th.—Turn the cotton once round the mesh, and net a stitch ; repeat all round ; when the mesh is withdrawn these loops will be double the length of the previous stitches.

30th.—Net every two stitches together ; then 2 rounds plain, and draw up the remaining stitches, fastening them firmly. Take it off the foundation, and run an elastic in the first round.

INVISIBLE NET.

Materials.—Fine sewing silk, or that known as "Invisible" silk ; a flat mesh, a quarter of an inch in width ; and a steel netting needle.

Commence on a foundation of 16 stitches (this will make a large size), and net 32 rows plain, working backwards and forwards ; take it off the foundation and stretch it open, when it will forma square, which is for the centre of the net ; a foundation thread must therefore be run along the four sides of it a few stitches from the edge. Net along the four sides, working 2 stitches in each of the corners ; then net 20 rounds plain, and fasten off. After the first 4 rounds are worked, it is advisable to run the foundation thread into the first of them, which will keep the netting even.

GODEY'S LADY'S BOOK
FEBRUARY 1864

CHITCHAT UPON NEW YORK AND PHILADEL-PHIA FASHION.

Small nets are now made for waterfalls which are found exceedingly convenient. They are of a very fine silk, either black or the color of the hair. Indeed, nets of any kind are still in vogue, some very highly trimmed with flowers, lace, or ribbon, for dinner or small companies, some of bright colors, forming the Scottish plaids. While white nets of a strong cotton, or, what is still better, a flat linen bobbin, have now taken the place of the night-cap. They answer every purpose, indeed, a better purpose, for the head is kept much cooler, the hair is kept in place, and the pillow-cases are not soiled by the grease of the hair—the last a great item in the consideration of housekeepers. For Invalids, nothing can be nicer than these white nets, which can be made quite tasteful by running a bright ribbon through them, and tying it either on top or at the side of the head. Merely a bow on top relieves them, and is very pretty. This certainly is an improvement on the night-cap, which seldom enhances the beauty of any one, but frequently detracts from their natural good looks. These nets are to be had of all sizes for children and ladies.

GODEY'S LADY'S BOOK
JUNE 1864

CHITCHAT UPON NEW YORK AND PHILADEL-PHIA FASHIONS FOR JUNE.

Nets are still in vogue for *demie toilettes*, and those formed of straw, or plaid chenille and ribbons, are among the newest. They are generally trimmed in the coronet style and are quite dressy.

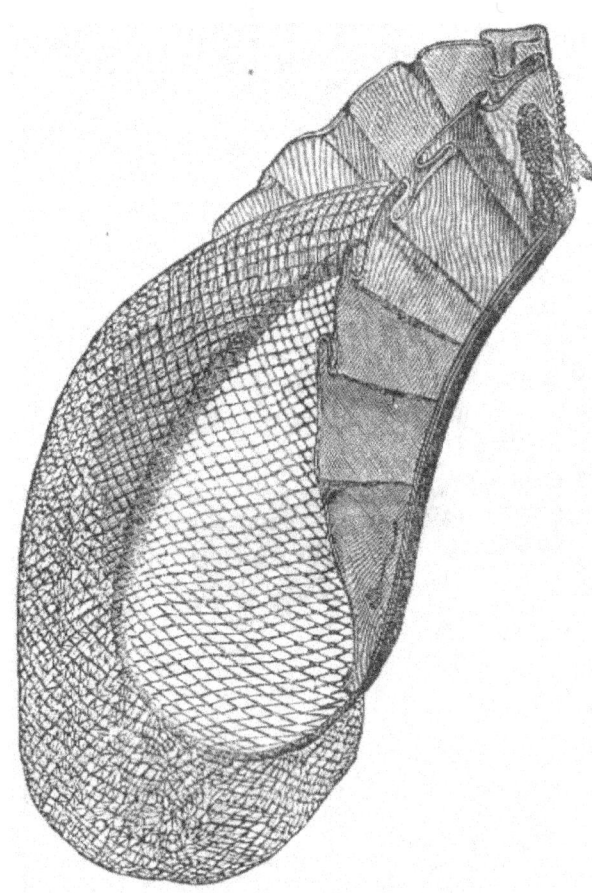

NOVELTIES FOR JULY

Fig. 15.—Hair net with ribbon coronet.

The materials are very fine sewing silk ; 1 yard 7 inches of ribbon, 3 inches wide ; one-half a yard of silk elastic ; 3 gimp ornaments ; a little black velvet ; a wooden mesh.

The foundation is netted in silk of the same shade as the hair, or else of any bright color.

Cast on 33 stitches, and net 34 rows, backwards and forwards. Around this square work 17 rows ; in the first of these 17 rows net 2 stitches in each stitch at the corners. Gather the piece of netting all round, work a small hem round the edge, and run through it a piece of silk elastic, and sew the ends together. To trim the net, first make with stiff black net a circle, not closed, about 12 inches long and one-half an inch wide. Run some fine wire into each edge of this circle ; bind it with a strip of black velvet, cut on the cross 2 1/2 inches wide, and sewn on so that it may be turned back on the outside over the trimming to hide the seam.

The trimming is arranged in the shape of a diadem ; it is finished in a point at each side, and forms five double pleats in front, each about 1 1/2 inch wide. On each side of these five pleats three plain ones are made, folded towards the back ; the pleats should cease about 3 1/2 inches from the end of the ribbon, at which place the ribbon is folded on the cross so as to terminate in a point. Place this diadem on the edge of the circle, between the wire and the velvet, which turn back and sew on the ribbon. Round the inside of the circle sew the net, plain, and even stretched a little, so that it may set well to the head. On the three middle pleats fasten three gimp ornaments ; these may be omitted if the net is preferred more simple.

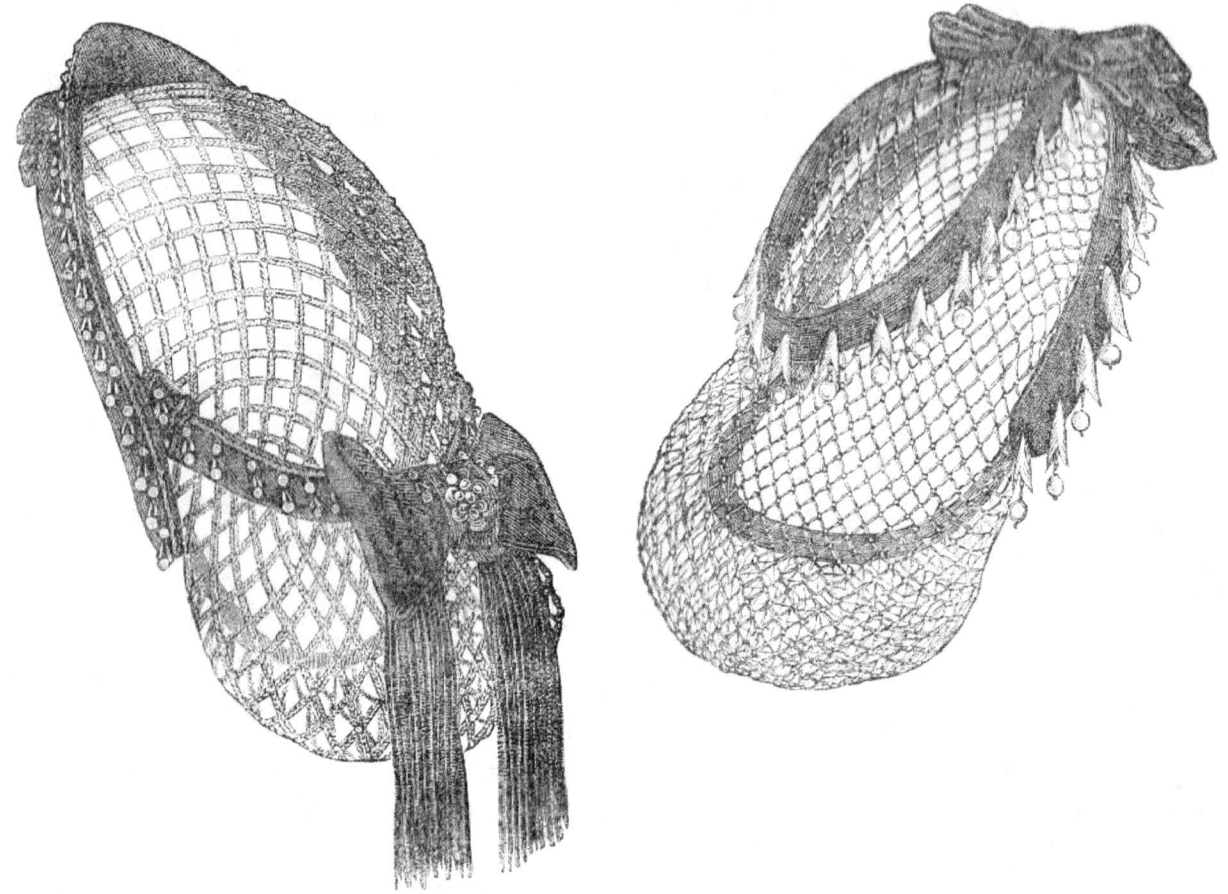

THE IMPERIAL NET COIFFURE.—
The diadem of crimson velvet, with a fringe of
straw and gold beads ; a straw rosette in the
centre of bow behind ; ends of chenille fringe.

GENERAL REMARKS.—Nets for young ladies
are made entirely of small coral beads, with a
flower, which harmonizes in color, at the side
of the head For example, if the net is red, a
red velvet orchid is added ; if it is worked with

THE "CORONA" NET COIFFURE.—
Trimmed with blue velvet on which are set
little bell-flowers of corn-colored silk, with
pendant crystal beads.

pearls, either a frosted rose or narcissus will be
selected.

GODEY'S LADY'S BOOK
APRIL 1865

CHITCHAT UPON NEW YORK AND PHILADELPHIA FASHIONS FOR APRIL.

Beads enter largely into the decorations of the present day, and when artistically mounted, are really very effective and beautiful. Some are, quite costly, being of malachite, pink, or red coral, amber, and frosty-looking crystal. All these are employed for headdresses, particularly for the trimming of nets. The invisible nets which are now woven as fine as hair, are not generally trimmed. The more showy and elaborate kinds form the most effective of coiffures. They are generally very large, and adorned with immense pearl, jet, steel, or crystal beads. The most elegant have a double row of beads forming a coronet in front, while a fringe of beads with pendent ends falls at the back.

GODEY'S LADY'S BOOK
MAY 1865

CHITCHAT UPON NEW YORK AND PHILADELPHIA FASHIONS FOR MAY.

Nets of all kinds are worn. Some of the newest are covered with steel or gilt spangles, or else large crystal beads.

GODEY'S LADY'S BOOK
AUGUST 1865

CHITCHAT UPON NEW YORK AND PHILADELPHIA FASHIONS FOR AUGUST.

Mme. Tilman, of 147 East Ninth Street, New York, has some very beautiful varieties of nets suitable both for full and *demie toilette*. Some are of very fine silk, studded with immensely large beads of pearl, gilt, jet, pink and red coral, malachite, bright and dull steel. The latter resembles lead, but is a pretty novelty. Others are of gold-colored silk covered with tiny pendent arrows or crescents. A very graceful style is of twisted gold and braid, every cross-bar being ornamented with small beads.

PETERSON'S MAGAZINE
OCTOBER 1865

GENERAL REMARKS.—THE NETS for evening wear are made either of invisible silk or of hair. Neither of these materials conceals the beauty of the hair; a coronet of velvet, on a twisted roll of fancy straw, is fastened to the net and worn at the top of the forehead. For young girls, these coronets are composed of loops of ribbon—velvet, or silk, according to the taste—as these are more youthful-looking than the heavier coronets. Aureoles of small rosettes made of narrow black ribbon velvet, edged with white, are also much worn with nets made of the same ribbon. Mauve nets are composed likewise in the way, and are very popular.

A NET AND NECKLACE, ORNAMENTED WITH CRYSTAL BEADS.—The necklace known in fashionable style as the "Collier Mignon" is formed of a band of blue silk, studded with crystal beads, and edged with a fringe of the same. It is finished off at the back with three loops and two long ends of blue ribbon. The ends are fringed with beads. The net covers the chignon only. It is made of very fine blue silk, and ornamented with rows of crystal beads, of graduated size. At the top there is a bow, formed of two loops and ends of blue velvet, trimmed with crystal beads and small stars.

Sources

Godey's Lady's Book. Publisher Louis A. Godey. Editor Mrs. Sarah J. Hale. Philadelphia.
Volumes LX.-LXXI. 1860-1865

Harper's New Monthly Magazine. Harper & Brothers, Publishers. New York. Volume XXIX.
October, 1864

The Lady's Friend. Publisher Deacon & Peterson. Editor Mrs. Henry Peterson. Philadelphia.
Volume II. 1865

The Lady's Home Magazine. Publisher T. S. Arthur & Co. Editors T.S. Arthur and Miss Virginia
F. Townsend. Volumes XV and XVI. 1860

Peterson's Magazine. Publisher Charles J. Peterson. Philadelphia. Volumes XXXVII.-XLVIII.
1860-1865

Timely Tresses

In 2006, Timely Tresses emerged from the creative endeavors of Mandy Foster and Dannielle Perry. The company has published 21 original patterns based on extant bonnets and antique fashion plates, 18 fashion plate books, and 3 millinery guides. For more information, visit www.timelytresses.com.